MW00638367

I Want What She's Got!

THE SECRETS OF CREATING AN OUTRAGEOUS LIFE

Debby,

You are so precious to our Father. Your outrageous life is still in front of you!

Enjoy!! Grab it all!!

Blessings!

Bette Laughrun

BETTE JAMES LAUGHRUN & KATHIE NELSON

FOREWORD BY BRIAN KLEMMER

Copyright 2010 Bette James Laughrun and Kathie Nelson
All rights reserved
Printed in the United States of America

No part of this book may be reproduced or transmitted in any form or by any means, electronic or mechanical, including photocopying and recording, or by an information storage and retrieval system, without permission in writing from the authors.

ISBN: 978-0-9826665-8-6
SELF-HELP / PERSONAL GROWTH / SUCCESS

Published by PCG Legacy, a division of Pilot Communications Group, Inc. 317 Appaloosa Trail Waco, TX 76712
www.thepublishinghub.com

HOW TO REACH THE AUTHORS:
www.IWantWhatShesGotSecrets.com

What Others Are Saying

"Bette proves that anyone who puts their mind, energy, passion, and focus into something they believe in, magic will happen. This is an example of the unlimited possibilities we all have. You are a role model for others to follow. Thank you for setting the pace."
— Kathy Coover, Executive Vice President, Isagenix® International LLC

This is a bestseller! It's motivational and inspirational, it'll make you laugh and cry, and it will also make you think. So many can relate who've fallen victim to "settling" for what life's dished them. Bette's story will inspire others to investigate their purpose and live life to the fullest, to the very end. This masterpiece is action packed and an easy read … one you can't put down! I am honored to know Bette as a friend, business partner, and spiritual mentor. Bette is a woman who loves the Lord and lives her life to honor Him. A true example. I am blessed to be part of her life and look forward to many more years of wild fun and prosperous times. You are truly an inspiration to so many … an example to follow.
— Patty Cepeda, business coach, author, www.ibelieveyoucan.com

"In the years that I have known Bette, I have always found her to be one of the most authentic and real people that I know. Her authenticity definitely shines in this book. I have watched Bette's growth over the past few years and her transition has been no less than amazing. She is truly living a dream life and is an inspiration to us all! I know that many will read Bette's story and know that they, too, can begin the journey to their best life!"
— Renata Lee, Isagenix Leader

"This is a must read for women who need to know and understand there is life after divorce."
— Vonnet Lephiew, Administrative Director, Women of Wealth and Worth Transformational Events, azwomenofworth.com

It's not very often that your dear friend becomes an author. When I first heard that Bette had been asked to write her story, my heart leapt for joy, for I knew her story. An amazing story that only grew over the years. *Ordinary* was never in her vocabulary, *challenge* meant just that and *passion* has always been forefront to her goals. As I read her rough draft, well into the night, I knew that I could not be the critic but prayed that I also could glean again from her experiences and learn from her lessons. One of the thrills of my life was the privilege of traveling with her to Israel. It will be forever marked in my heart, her compassion and amazing love for God's special people and His special land. It was my honor to travel by her side. As you read this book, I pray that you will see the amazing value that God has placed on you and that you will pick up the challenge to be all that God has intended you to be. As you read her book you will see that circumstances must not rule the victory. Read on!
— Carol Wall, Albany Oregon

Contents

I want what she's got

Acknowledgments

I've learned it takes a lot of people to make a book come together. I am humbled as I remember the connections and contributions of those along the way.

Most important is to give thanks to God. It is His gift and enabling that makes it possible for us to live with purpose and contribute to our world. This "cracked pot" is grateful for the treasure inside (2 Cor. 4:7).

First and foremost, thanks to my daughters, Patsi Day and Kathie Nelson, who have been there for me as encouragers and supporters in every way they could. To Patsi for always helping make things work at home and in business (dinners, laundry, bookkeeping, legal work, and more). To Kathie for her invaluable coaching, mentoring, and collaboration to create this book. What a privilege to have two such talented and capable women in my family.

For my son, David, who has been a support extraordinaire. He made us laugh and kept our focus on the right things. He is an amazing person and an incredible son.

For Dolores Day, a special thanks for doing what I consider to be one of the hardest jobs of all. She took my ramblings from a tape recorder and set me on the path to a "real" book through hours of transcription.

For Kim Greenwood, a most delightful and highly skilled copy editor. She made the book sing when I couldn't describe my experiences. She pushed me to do what most authors do naturally, to bring more to the table than sauerkraut and bean salad.

For Nancy Juetten, who suggested a version of this title for the book when I attended one of her "DIY Publicity Workshops." The gift of this title kept us smiling and focused as we birthed this book.

My dear friend Judy Campbell, who has been my trusted prayer partner and listening post. She has always known I could do this even when I didn't think I could.

Rich Chrono, Level IV Business Coaching — thanks for pushing me and prodding me because you believed there was a book inside of me. You helped me believe it myself and started me on the road to make it a reality.

Foreword

Have you ever met someone who does something that surprises you and you say, "Wow, I didn't know you had it in you?" It may be a quiet friend who is a hilarious comedian on stage, a flighty neighbor who writes the most thought-provoking articles you've ever read, or a nerdy kid who turns out to be an entrepreneurial genius.

To a certain degree, this is all of us. People can't tell who we really are or what we will become by their first meeting of us. That is precisely why we need to give others room to grow, to be themselves, and to chart their own course.

When I was first introduced to Bette Laughrun, I had no idea what was inside of her. How could I? We had just met, but I have learned from experience that if I give people a fresh glimpse of their potential, many will grab hold of their dreams with renewed passion and will go on to accomplish the impossible.

When Bette and I crossed paths, a little over 10 years ago, she had almost given up on herself and on her dreams. The fire of hope was flickering, but it was still there, and through our time together, something happened inside of her. The lights came on, and she was off.

And now, 10 years later, Bette has penned words that will change tens, hundreds, and even thousands of lives! Of that there is no question.

Whatever is in you, whatever dream you have not yet achieved, I challenge you to recharge (not burnout), to refire (not retire), and to revive (not let die) what is within you.

Bette is an incredible example, and the insights within these pages come from years and years of experience. May these pages add fuel to your fire, today and for years to come.

— Brian Klemmer, Klemmer & Associates

7 Questions Every Woman Must Answer to Create an Outrageous Life

Time is all we have. Our relationships are critical. At the end of the day, we only have one life to live. We are born wired to love, innately geared to thrive with a homing beacon that draws us to be more ... to become that person we were created to be. The longing for significance, to contribute, to have deep relationships is essential to our fulfillment factor.

The content of this book is dedicated to inspiring you to define and choose your own outrageous, over-the-top life ... and motivate you to LIVE it. As you read you will have time to reflect on these clarifying questions. Before you are done reading, check out the Outrageous Life Design Tool in Chapter 9.

The seven questions you must ask and answer ...

1. The Question of *Purpose*

— Why am I here? What's my purpose? What is my legacy?

11

2. The Question of *Gift Mix*

— What talents or value can I bring to the party besides my famous Jell-O salad?

3. The Question of *Relationships*

— How can I make the time I spend with friends and family count? What's missing in my relationships? How can I make a difference?

4. The Question of *Contribution*

— Beyond working day in and day out, warming the couch cushions, watching the grandkids and playing bridge, how can I make a difference in the world?

5. The Question of *Self Care*

— How does my health affect my outlook and energy? What can I do about it? Do I take the time to do what I need to do for me?

6. The Question of *Vision*

— Beyond what I can see with my bifocals — what's in store for the rest of my life? At the end of my life (which isn't now) what do I want those around me to say about me? Is there something that stirs my heart, but I think I am too old to accomplish? Who's telling me I can't? Why?

7. The Question of *Spirituality*

— What does spirituality mean to me? How does it make a difference in my life? What are my core values? How do they guide me?

You are an amazing person. You are used to multi tasking, ball juggling, baby wrangling, car pooling, organizing, and managing a whirlwind of tasks that come your way. This is your chance to think about YOU.

Let yourself imagine what an outrageous over-the-top life would be for you. Have fun!

Chapter One

Life Is
a Choice

Have you settled for less than your dream?

I just returned from a dream vacation where I spent a full week enjoying the blue skies, ocean breezes, azure water, white sands, and colorful tropical fish. Even better, I enjoyed this dream vacation with my children and their children. It was paradise!

At the close of this trip, I paused to revisit each memory. Savoring every moment, my heart overflowed with love and gratitude. The significance of this situation was intensified by the awareness that I could have missed it all!

Ten years ago this once-in-a-lifetime opportunity to create new memories and re-build relationships under sunny skies with sand between our toes, would have been nothing more than a fantasy. And yet here I was, creating a new legacy of joy, living life to the fullest and embracing an outrageous life of love and fulfillment. But getting to this sandy beach was a long journey. Like every journey, it started with the first step.

You see, my family had scattered across the United States 25 years earlier after the final dissolution of my marriage. My children, ranging from 17 to 28 years in age, each responded to the change in relationship in their own way. Instead of coming together as a family to work through this life-altering change, we all found it easier to retreat and moved to our own corners of the country.

I had settled in ... and I was waiting to die.

Personally, I was worn down after years of trying to find where I fit and wear the roles people assigned me — none of them really fitting who I was. My long-time dream of a united, happy family was more like a fairy tale than anything else.

I had settled for a reality so different than what I truly wanted, I didn't even see how far I had drifted from my heart's desire. Trying to put the pieces of my own life back together, on an impulse, I responded to an invitation to a personal development seminar[1] (at the age of 66 it was uncharacteristic of me to attend such a thing). I knew I needed to do something to spark a change in my life, but I just didn't have a clue where to start.

Sitting in the initial session of the workshop, I wondered, *What am even doing here? At my age isn't it really too late for these kinds of changes?* Followed by the thought, *Will this be worth the investment?*

Now, that's certainly not an uncommon question, except the real question underneath was, **Will I live long enough to realize the return?**

In one of the sessions, we were asked to share what we thought our purpose in life was. As I thought through this question, I suddenly realized I wasn't living with any purpose. I was simply living my life choosing to merely exist until death claimed me. Yes — I would go through the motions, attending events, checking in with the family, taking care of day-to-day activities, but it was all

---

[1] Personal Mastery Seminar, by Brian Klemmer www.klemmer.com

just an empty routine marking time until my life story reached "the end."

What a sad reality!

This surprising revelation came in the third in a series of seminars offered by Klemmer and Associates, a phenomenal leadership development company. I had already participated in "Personal Mastery," the workshop dealing with damaging belief systems that keep us from positive outcomes. This seminar helps participants understand that "programs," subconscious thought processes developed through our lives, impact our decisions.

These programs greatly influence our life and create patterns of behavior that are often unhealthy. If we don't pay attention, pretty soon our life is on autopilot and we can get lazy and just stop trying to make positive choices in our lives because it's so much easier to just follow our set patterns.

While many people at the event translated the message to their business opportunities, it was there I realized that I was the reason my grandchildren didn't relate to me. I didn't take time for or relate to them! Learning about these programs was my first step in redirecting my thinking and actively making choices in my life.

I went on to complete the "Advanced Leadership Seminar," a workshop that teaches participants to break up the damaging programs that run you and allow new choices to be available to you. This session gave me some ideas about how to begin to relate to my grandkids in a practical way. I hadn't had relationships with them for many years, mostly because busy lives kept it from being a priority.

I gained fresh insight into "busyness" as a program running in the background for many of us, including myself. It's easy to see how we allow our busyness to distract us while we slip into routines and patterns that keep us from connecting with our loved ones in meaningful ways. This was one of the first "programs" I decided to change. Building relationships with my grandchildren needed to be a priority.

In both the previous seminars, I figured I was short-term and didn't have a lot of time to invest so I quietly participated in what I could do with the time I thought I had left. When the seminar was over I shared, "If I die tomorrow the value I received from this workshop would have been worth it."

The third seminar in the Klemmer program is called "Heart of the Samarai" and focuses on contribution. I received a scholarship for this program or probably wouldn't have gone. By the end of the week, even though I saw lots of value and participated in events, I was unchanged in my outlook and expectation of a limited lifespan.

It was at this point the leader asked what my purpose was. I struggled to think of something but I was blank. I didn't have an answer except that my purpose was to wait for my own death. I was unaware of anyone else's response since mine shook me to my core. *How could I have had this outlook on my life for these recent years and not seen it for what it was?*

This realization shocked and surprised me. Looking back on my life, I wondered if I had ever fully lived. Of course I had lived from moment to moment, phase to phase. Five children and marriage kept my attention until they were gone, but here was my world: after years of living out whatever purpose lay in front of me at each stage of life, in the end I was left with grown children, no husband, and a lack of direction.

Without realizing it, this had become the way I was living my life. I had settled in, given up my dreams, and I was convinced my only path was to wait — living the rest of my life in a perpetual holding pattern.

The Power of the Mind

My daughter, Patsi, lived nearby. We decided to relocate to the Western Slope of Colorado and when I voiced the idea of moving from my current home she suggested that I live right next door so she could be there to take care of me when I got older and needed assistance. (I was grateful for her sensitive heart, but these kinds of conversations only served to reinforce my "end of life" mindset.)

Like many people, I found myself marking my life benchmarks against those of my parents. My mom was 74 and my dad was 68 when they died. At 66, I calculated that I had only around two to eight more years to live! Knowing in my head this was seriously flawed logic, the belief in my heart that this would be my fate was a powerful influence in my life. That belief was subtle yet it seeped into my daily decisions and kept me from really living!

It wasn't the truth, but because I believed it, it was real to me.

Where did such a dismal view of life come from? It came so naturally. All it took was a friend's casual comment, "People can usually expect a life span of within a few years of their parents." This made sense and I bought into the lie. Like a bramble vine left unchecked in a garden of dreams, this thorny thought of a shortened life started to choke out the dreams and plans I had already neglected for so much of my life.

It wasn't long before they were buried by this invasive thought pattern: *Don't make too many plans, Bette! You don't have much time left!*

After a lifetime of "settling" for less than my dreams and desires, this thought pattern had fertile soil to grow in. I found myself participating in a series of non-productive day-to-day activities.

Sitting at the "Heart of the Samurai" seminar, I learned that your frame of mind shapes all the decisions you make. Think about it — what do you do when you feel you don't have much time left? What plans do you make? How much do you invest in life if you don't believe you'll be there to reap your return?

As a result of this fatalistic mindset, I weighed everything: friendships, studying, challenging myself, money spent, etc. Everything was placed on a scale and evaluated by the return on the investment.

As ridiculous as it sounds, after a dental appointment, I rejected the idea of having an eyetooth replaced after an extraction. The procedure was expensive. *Why spend money on it?* I thought to myself. *What's the point? I won't live long enough to enjoy it.*

My thoughts were solely focused on how I could make my short time left on earth easier for me and everyone else. My big plan was to fade into the sunset saving others any hardship or difficulty. How's that for small mindedness? I didn't realize how wrong I was!

Life definitely changes when you think you're dying. There was no need for long-range planning. No need to promote my business. No reason to plant a tree. No motivation to think about others and no more expectations.

It wasn't the truth, but because I believed it, it was real to me. I had no way of knowing that I started to die inside when I lost my purpose.

It wasn't the truth,
but because
I believed it,
it was real to me.

Considering my reality

During the course of the seminar, I had a chance to take stock of my current reality. I could see that I had a lot going for me. These seminars are interactive. Each part has an exercise designed to cause you to remember and take stock of your resources. Personal reflection is critical to understanding the areas that need changing in our lives.

My life changed when I got back "in the game."

While reflecting on the good, you also take time to look at the hard things and review their affect on your life. This is an incredibly powerful exercise that provides tremendous insight to see how we inadvertently make decisions based on inaccurate information.

I had:
- excellent health
- five terrific kids
- seven wonderful grandchildren
- many great things that I enjoyed in life
- traveled extensively
- involvement in a ministry I cared deeply about
- loyal friends
- a thriving business

Looking at my list I could see just how blessed I really was. In that moment of introspection and gratitude, I thought to myself, *I am thankful for the life I have lived and will be okay to just disappear….*

Suddenly the fuzzy image of my life started to come into focus. I could now see how I had bought into the lie that I would only have about the same life expectancy as my parents. I could see how I had been filtering every one of my choices through this lie.

As a result, I wasn't living with any purpose or vision and avoided anything that looked like an investment of time, energy or money. I'd been acting as if I was already a dead woman!

21

When I left the seminar I was shaken and surprised at this realization. Though it was subconscious, I had been making choices based on a false premise — I was living my life based on a lie, and that lie was controlling my decisions and emotions.

With utmost clarity, I suddenly decided, *I **have** to make a new choice!*

I could choose to die or I could choose to live. It was up to me. It was my choice.

At that moment, I made an abrupt 180-degree turn and determined to reconnect to life. I chose to live! To really live — until I die. It didn't matter if I died tomorrow, from this day forward, I would change my focus from dying to really living. My choice!

My new premise: I have choices!

Once the decision was made to choose life, it was like coming back from the grave. I determined to be a part of my world whenever possible. I wanted to participate. I wanted to be "with" people, in the moment, instead of merely observing. I longed to serve others in meaningful ways, to play, and to contribute. It was like deciding to walk again. Once you begin, you can start to skip, then run and then switch into overdrive to give it all you've got.

How you respond to life ... is your choice.

It was not long after this shift in my thinking that I began to more fully engage with life ... and things began to happen! Going 120 miles an hour, here I come!! Like a breath of fresh air, I wanted to taste and experience life like never before. I began to embrace the heart of this old saying:

"Life is not a journey to the grave with the intention of arriving safely in a pretty and well preserved body, but rather to skid in broadside, thoroughly used up,

22

totally worn out, and loudly proclaiming, WOW!!!!
What a ride!" — *Author unknown*

One aspect of my life that saw immediate improvements from my new-found focus and energy was my business. I was already an associate in an international nutritional cleansing company. I had been using the products to improve my health and weight a few years earlier. I had experienced some success with the business, but nothing like I found when I launched a campaign to develop other leaders with a passion to make a difference in the world.

This new vision and purpose led to many of my dreams realized, including the reunion of my family. Financial rewards from finding a new purpose in my work life helped make that dream Hawaiian vacation with my family a reality.

This magical trip took place over 19 years after the dissolution of my family. We spent the week making wonderful new memories together, healing past wounds and rebuilding the bonds of love and trust in our family. I am in awe at how this dream was made a reality all because I made the choice to live.

Where choices will take you

Through experiences of success and failure, I have learned that my vision of the future and the premise on which I base my choices can propel me forward or limit me to a life of mediocrity. It's up to me! I get to choose which it will be.

What woke me up was a simple question. Someone at the seminar basically asked me, "What do you want to be when you grow up?" I was 66 years old ... and had never answered that question!

I could see that up to this point I had been making choices based on a flawed belief system that my productive life was over and I had no real purpose. My life changed when I chose to get back "in the game." By shifting my focus from **waiting to die** to **making my**

life count something wonderful happened. I started rebuilding my legacy.

This was the start of my truly outrageous life! I understand from the depths of my heart that what I am experiencing now, less than a decade later, is a direct result of the choices I have made based on my new premise: that my choices affect my destiny.

My life changed when I got back "in the game."

What about you?

I don't want you to wait another minute to get the outrageous life you deserve. Not all of you have the resources or time to attend leadership conferences, but you can still benefit from the practice of reflecting on your life and answering some action-provoking questions.

At the end of each chapter, there will be some questions to help you think about where you are and where you want to be. Taking the time to reflect and answer them honestly can help you find your own choices that will move you forward in your journey to an outrageous life.

1. What do you hope for in your future?

2. What do you want to be when you "grow up"?

3. What choices are keeping you from living an outrageous life?

My life changed when I chose to engage. It's your life, your choice. What will you choose?

"Set before you is life and death .... So choose life in order that you may live." (Deut. 30:19)

Chapter Two

Outrageous Living Is Supernatural

Have you ever felt like you lived an invisible existence? There was a time in my life where I felt I walked around like a ghost in my own home.

Everyday life has its ups and downs but I had sunk into the most desperate low of my life. At age 32, I was totally discouraged and despairing of ever seeing a better future. I loved my kids but I was convinced my husband had no interest in me other than to criticize the way I made dinner, and to make babies for him. I didn't understand his love language and wasn't able to receive the love he was trying to communicate to me.

Facing life — this life — I was empty. Invisible. There was no hope of my own fulfillment.

Life as a military wife meant we were constantly on the move, zigzagging across the U.S., always starting over, trying to develop new relationships. None of us could make lasting relationships so it was like we were always on a new adventure. There were a few exceptions.

Over time we found some friendships that stuck — often with others who shared our transient lifestyle. They say that military wives always have a great life 50% of the time. Either the time their husbands are home or when they are gone.

Today, the military does extensive counseling and provides support and resources for families separated for long periods, but in the 1960s they didn't realize how at-risk we were. The stresses of raising the children in this kind of life and the prolonged separations from my husband had wrung me out.

When my husband was home, we fought continually for control of the home. I had to be in control when he was gone and it was hard to relinquish that power when he returned.

When we were together, the family dynamics created by two people from totally different backgrounds only reinforced my feelings of inadequacy and desperation. Between the two of us, to others I actually appeared to have the stronger personality, but my husband, Floyd, ruled our world, and I complied, pushing my own needs and desires further and further away from the reality of my life.

Who's really been in charge?

Growing up, I knew I could always manipulate my parents. They loved me, but they never knew how to stand up to my strong-willed behavior. As a result, I ruled — they didn't. Going into marriage, my history was a scattered wreck of relationships. I had desperately sought out people in my life who could help me set boundaries but I always managed to pull back and push them away.

I knew there was something unbalanced in these patterns, always being the stronger personality, the one who called the shots. I knew I wanted someone to partner with — not rule over, but old patterns, programs, and selfish motives seemed to always win in the end.

I stumbled over my own poor choices in relationships resulting in a marriage at age 16, giving birth to a son at 17, receiving an annulment at 18, followed by the birth of a daughter who I gave up for adoption. The consequences of my choices made me grow up quickly. I was forced to make some tough decisions early in my life based on these early mistakes. I really did try to learn from them and live responsibly, but I was so out of control due to my own needs not being met that I often made choices that fell far short of what I intended.

When I first met Floyd, I could tell he was a strong individual. He was painfully shy around girls, but there was a strength that showed through in the way he carried himself. He decided to take some dancing lessons at Arthur Murray Dance Studio because he was so shy he didn't have much of a social life with women. I was 20 and working as a dance instructor, and I was drawn to this handsome young sailor.

Looking back is essential to understanding where you are.

He was in a leadership position on his submarine where he carried a lot of responsibility. His team all seemed to admire and respect him. As we started to spend time together, I probed his co-workers for information about this quiet man. I didn't realize it at the time, but I was in a sense interviewing them to see if Floyd would be the person I could make a life with. I was looking for an answer to a need that I didn't realize I had.

In my search for someone who would provide boundaries and finally challenge my desire to always be in control, I found it in Floyd. On our first date, he didn't like the way I had put on my makeup and told me, "go home and wash your face." I was shocked but also impressed. I decided at that moment that I would marry him. No one had ever talked to me like that before.

In my search for someone to provide boundaries, I ended up thinking this kind of influence would help me. I didn't realize at the time how it would eventually chip away at my heart and soul leaving raw and jagged edges. There would be enough blame for both of us to share, but this kind of dysfunctional relationship would cause so many problems in our future. At that time, I felt like Floyd was the answer to all of my problems; someone to control me and rescue me from the life of destructive choices I had been making.

Six weeks after we first met, he came back from a tour passing over the equator and we were married. With his freshly shaved head as an initiation rite, and his handsome Navy uniform, he embodied the image of the leadership qualities I was looking for: A good, strong leader for our family who would help me stay in the boundaries my parents never could.

Marrying in haste and out of need is not a wise or safe place to be, but I didn't know it at the time. I quickly learned two broken people don't make a whole couple. This is wisdom I wish I could have shared with my younger self to save her from years of heartache and sadness, and yet, it's the kind of truth you can only learn by pulling back the veil yourself. No voice could have shouted loud enough to sway my young self from the path I was so sure would bring happiness and security after a series of choices that had brought grief and loss.

From different worlds

Almost before the petals fell from my wedding day flowers, it was clear we were very different people. Floyd came from a family of nine and grew up in the hills of Eastern Tennessee. His parents had a small farm in a "hollow" and he lived with no electricity or luxuries in his home. He walked miles to school with no shoes. (It was uphill both ways as I remember the story.)

He left home and joined the Navy at the age of 17. He just wanted to get away from the life he had experienced. He was deeply connected with pain and dysfunction as the middle child of nine kids trying to survive during the Depression. He had a deep love of the earth, wanted a large family, a farm and most importantly, he equated hard work and provision as an expression of his love. He gave the best that he had to give. We were warm, fed, and secure.

I was raised in the city of Los Angeles as the oldest of two. I was the first grandchild and along with a few natural talents, enjoyed the role as the golden child. I spent my growing up years living summers with my grandparents in Los Angeles and during the school year, I lived in Northern California with my parents. We had a house on a paved street with a white picket fence around it. My parents were both college graduates and mom wasn't a working mother. My dad had a prestigious position as a chemist and rubber technologist for the government.

With a active social and professional life that kept them busy, I went to private schools as a teenager so my parents could try to keep me "in hand." They just didn't know how to deal with a child who didn't conform and kept slipping out of their grasp. Before marrying Floyd, I had no experience with tending the earth and "hard work" was not in my vocabulary. Add the fact that I wanted a small family and anyone but a teenager in love could see we were headed for trouble.

Did I have expectations? I had plenty of them! My vision of marriage and being a wife was shaped by Ginger Rogers/Fred Astaire movies, the Cleaver family on TV, and Tony Curtis and Janet Leigh — the stars in that era who modeled fairy-tale romances and ideal marriages. Shows with smiles, laughter, conversations, families together — working through problems between commercials and always ending the day/show with an affectionate word or look that said "everything will be all right" were my models for marriage and parenting. It always looked like so much fun and the "romance" of these images created a longing in a lonely teenager.

Boy, what a setup for failure for a real-life relationship!

These distinct differences in personality and values between us made life complicated. They continually reinforced the feeling that I could never be what he needed me to be and he could never be what I wanted him to be.

Floyd had his own list of expectations:

- ✔ I was to keep things spic and span
- ✔ I was to produce consistent meals
- ✔ the main meal was to be meat-and-potatoes
- ✔ I was to preserve all the produce he grew
- ✔ And more … (I never got past the first ones)

It wasn't long before I dutifully put on the uniform of wife, mother, cook, and housekeeper. I wore it moderately well and from the outside, I came across as a loving wife, supporting her husband and doing her best to live the dream of so many young girls.

But inside my heart and soul I was crying out, "I want to be more than a cook, housekeeper, and a baby-making machine! I want love and I am not getting it here. I want more!"

At the end of my rope

After 12 long years, feeling unappreciated and devalued in my home and frustrated in my child rearing, I couldn't bear it any longer. One night, falling into bed exhausted (as mothers often do) I whispered to God, "Please remind me to talk to you in the morning because if I don't, I'm just not sure what I'll do."

The next day, I got up and did all the usual morning chores — making breakfasts, packing lunches, clearing the dishes and tidying up, getting my husband off to work and the kids off to school. As I wiped down a counter in the quiet of my now empty kitchen, I stopped in my tracks as I remembered my unfinished conversation with God.

Overwhelmed by a deep sadness, I dissolved into tears. Sitting at my kitchen table, feeling like I was hanging on to the edge of a cliff by my fingernails, in desperation I cried out, "God, if you don't help me, I'm ready to quit. If you're really there, I need you now!"

I knew that God valued me — even in the mess I was in — and that changed me.

I found myself reaching out to a something or someone bigger than myself and my circumstance. Going through the motions of a busy life, I had become a shell. Constantly torn between giving to and loving my family and hating what they brought out in me — feelings of worthlessness made me want to escape and left me broken. I knew I was inadequate for the job and there was no more hope for me.

I couldn't seem to measure up and didn't even know how to. I had jumped into this wife-and-mother role with no training and the façade was starting to crack. My thoughts turned to dark places of ending my life and ending the misery. Inside, my soul screamed, "I can't live another day like this!" I was totally at the end of my resources.

The deep knowing that my life wasn't working had finally brought me to my knees. I started to recognize that as a strong-willed young woman, I had directed my own life (or tried to) since the age of three. I began to acknowledge that little girl, crossing her arms and stomping her feet within me, furrowing her eyebrows, letting out a loud and frustrated wail of, "Stop it!"

Living my life was like facing down a bully, one who was constantly poking me where it hurt, tripping me just as I was reaching a good stride, pushing me down in the dust, and kicking pebbles at me as it moved on by. She was tired. I was tired. Tired

31

of seeing happiness dangled in front of me and then having it snatched away. Tired of a lifetime of disappointments carried like stones in a backpack. Tired of the constant battle to be strong, when I felt so weak.

At that moment, when I'd reached the limits of my own strength, God met me. Something changed in me. I knew it. I felt it deep within my being. There was a certain moment in that prayer to God where a shift occurred. I sensed that I was heard, valued, and complete, and it was as if God came and soothed all my hurts, filled all the holes, and replaced them with His peace and truth. He picked me up and brushed me off and it was as if His presence was enough to cause the bully to run for cover. I finally felt love for the first time. I knew my parents loved me and now know that my husband did, too. I just hadn't ever been able to receive real love.

New life, new heart, new direction

For days, all I could feel was love. Not yet ready to articulate this life-changing experience to my family, it needed some sort of expression. The outlet came in the act of cleaning my house. I mean really cleaning my house. All the love and life giving presence that had cleaned the wounds of my heart came out in the act of scrubbing floors, and every wall I washed down was an expression of love to my family and how loved I felt. It was a total transformation.

Self-focused lives are rarely outrageous.

For an entire week I cleaned and gave back the best I had to give. It was like love was a warm bath that I just carried with me everywhere I went. Totally amazing.

I'm no theologian and I can't explain how that one moment brought about such a lasting change in my life, but something remarkable happened and a seed of faith was born in me. Inside,

I was new. The Bible verse *"old things have passed away and all things have become new"* (2 Corinthians 5:17) just sang to me. I knew those old verses and hymns because I had been to church and Sunday School as a child but they had never affected me in the way they now did.

I knew that God valued me — even in the mess I was in! Understanding that truth for the first time **changed me**. My self-absorption dissolved, my heartache subsided. I could see my situation with fresh eyes. Most importantly, I began looking outward instead of inward.

My family all noticed the change immediately and stood at a distance not really being able to believe it. They all wanted to wait and see if it would last because it was too good to be true.

More than just a shift in perspective, this experience caused me to act differently. It was as if I were alive for the first time. Even 40 years later, I remember it like it was yesterday. I could really understand the verses from the hymn, "Amazing Grace," that said, "I once was lost, but now am found, was blind, but now I see." I know it sounds impossible, but I know differently. The internal change I experienced that day was supernatural.

What makes me think so? It happened instantly without me having to create new habits that supported a new belief or develop a new thought system through efforts on my own, and the new me has been living in this reality for over 40 years now. I know without a doubt I could not have precipitated that kind of sudden yet lasting change on my own. My thoughts and motivations changed radically, and that kind of change doesn't happen from simply changing your mind.

Up to that point, I had called all the shots in my life. Not that I was outwardly controlling and manipulative, but I certainly looked out for my own interests, putting myself first. There was one adjective that would describe all my childhood and young adult life: selfish. The experience with God in my kitchen on that wonderful morning changed all that and opened the door to live a life that was meaningful and filled with purpose.

We want it our way

I'm not the only one who has struggled with living a self-absorbed life. Our society breeds a sense of entitlement that spreads faster than any virus known to the CDC. Many live by the code WIFM (What's In It for Me?). I certainly did. We rush to buy anyone or anything that promises us success-made-easy alternatives. We want life strategies, success principles, and get-rich-without-doing-any-work opportunities to be delivered to our doorstep without breaking a sweat.

It's all about what I want, how I want to run *my* life, about *my* success, and about *my* financial gain. These are all tools, tricks, and tactics that we think we can control to create a desired change.

The mere realization that you can have more and be more in life ... will set your heart on fire!

This is only natural, right? Shouldn't we all try to better ourselves? But if this were really the right path, even with all the formulas, insights, and information available to do things our way, why do so many people still end up struggling with mediocrity, self-doubt, and frustrated dreams?

All of our efforts seem to come up short. They did in my life until that day in my kitchen. God took my life of striving for selfish goals and changed my heart so I could see my life as He saw it — vibrant and full of vision. We can't even see the colors of our world until God opens our eyes. Everything looks different through His life in us.

If seeking a life devoted to the best for me were the answer, you would think we would have fewer problems, but there is a limit to how far, in our own strength, we can better ourselves. Why don't we just admit that we aren't succeeding and ask for help from the One who knows us better than anyone else? Is our pride so great that we can't let go and recognize we need help?

Does any of this sound familiar to you? Have you found yourself wondering why you can't seem to break habits or create lasting change in yourself?

I learned that an outrageous life doesn't happen naturally — it's not something we can implement like a 12-step plan or purchase like a new piece of equipment or software to make our lives better, faster, and stronger. In fact, there's an element of the outrageous life that isn't in our power at all. We can choose to do outrageous things that gain attention but the truly outrageous over-the-top life experience is beyond natural … it's "super" natural.

When I reached the end of myself, I gave up on the self-help solutions and cried out for something more. The suspicion buried deep in my heart, that I was designed for more — something greater than the life I had accepted — kept me seeking to find the truth. My simple act of crying out to God when I realized I could no longer "do" life on my own, flipped a switch within me. At that moment I realized there was more to life than just living for my own selfish desires for the perfect life and family. There was a greater purpose and now I knew I could find it.

It's your choice. Are you wondering if my answer might just work for you? Are you tired of trying to be someone you are not? Maybe like me, you're worn out with trying to make everyone happy and everything perfect relying only on your own strength. Or maybe you are ready to recognize that small voice inside that says you are destined for more.

I've learned since those early days you don't have to wait till you hit bottom to get beyond yourself. God says if you call on Him, He will come and show you great and mighty things.

Say "no" to mediocrity

We don't choose to live lives of mediocrity … we settle for them. Somehow we buy the lie that this is how life should be. We end up becoming people we didn't want to become. The forces that compel us to mediocrity press us from all sides. We are pressured to fit in our social environments, our families, our workplaces. To chart a different course takes intention and a willingness to follow the small voice within and discover the truth of your own destiny.

> "Two roads diverged in a wood and I — I took the one less traveled by, and that has made all the difference" — *Robert Frost*

You were created for something more than mediocrity. Regardless of your own faith journey, these principles still apply. When you value yourself and believe you are valued you will see the world with fresh eyes. Honor that inner voice within you that calls you to be something more, and don't settle for anything less than being who you were created to be. He is calling you to be His own, His cherished child to bring about amazing things in your future.

Feeding your soul is an important part of living the outrageous life. Journaling can be an excellent way to begin this journey. Write down your dreams and visions for the life you want to live: the one you really want — not the one Madison Avenue tries to sell you. Write down some of your favorite quotes or words that inspire you. Cut out photos from magazines or draw images that reflect the passions and desires inside you for the life you want to live. Perhaps Bible verses or quotes from other spiritual texts will encourage you to look for the super-natural ways you find the life you want to live. (Chapter 9 has an Outrageous Life Design Tool to walk you through the process.)

Along this path, I fervently pray you come to know the Creator of the Universe and understand He lovingly crafted you for the purpose to which He called you. You have undeniable and significant value and you deserve to live an outrageous life of joy!

My faith journey started 40 years ago. It has been the ride of a life-time. I can see now how I was always meant to be in this place. My choices, my beliefs, and my actions all worked together to propel or distract me from a fulfilled life as I navigated each phase.

I'm thankful to be here, and it's been supernatural, to say the least.

What about you?

Here are my questions for you:

1. Where in your life do you feel stuck?

2. In what areas are you settling for mediocrity?

3. If you could be anyone or do anything you want, what would it be?

If you haven't begun your journey of faith yet, do so now. If you've been trying really hard to be good, to do the "right" things, this may be your time to give it up. We encourage you to stop right now and ask God for help. More resources can be found in the back of the book.

Here is an excerpt from www.needhim.org to get you started right now:

How does the wall come down?

You cannot change the fact that Jesus died for you over 2,000 years ago. The sacrifice was made whether or not you choose to believe it. To accept the sacrifice is to receive life. To reject it is to negate the payment made on your behalf and to choose your own eternal death instead. The choice is yours.

Do you want the wall between you and God to come down? Do you want eternal life?

God wants to give you forgiveness and the promise of eternity as a free gift. Not because you tried hard enough and hit the mark of holy perfection, but because His son died on the cross so that He might see you as purified through the perfect sacrifice of Jesus.

So, it's a gift. And like any gift, it stays with the giver unless the receiver reaches out and takes it as his own. You must reach out and take forgiveness from the One who offers it. If you don't take it, it will never become yours.

What is amazing is that God accepts you right now, as you are. He has been waiting to joyfully welcome you home. You only need to take a step and acknowledge Him:

"God, I believe you are there. I want to know you more, even if it means I might have to change some things. Thank you for accepting me and forgiving me as I am."

Your journey has started! God is already speaking to your heart.

Chapter Three

The Cost of Love

Beep, beep, beep … the drone of the machines in the ICU wore on. Though her face was swollen and unrecognizable, it was my 23-year-old daughter lying on the bed, her body broken. A twisting chain of tubes and wires tethered her to machines keeping her alive. My eyes took in the massive metal superstructure holding her broken body together — her extremities wrapped with plaster, and her head wrapped with bandages. It was hard to recognize that this was my baby girl, and nearly impossible to comprehend that she was here, hanging onto life by a thread!

When I think of the most challenging times of my life this ranks at the top. Of all my children, Kathie has always seemed the most like me. My intense love for her was tinged with fear that she would repeat the life I had, making similar destructive choices. Here I was, standing by her side not knowing if she would live, much less recover to a normal life.

Our family gathered around, each of us processing this tragedy in our own way. Our fears wrestled with our faith. From the bottom of our hearts, we wanted to believe everything would be OK. Time slowed to a standstill as the days passed.

I had hugged Kathie that rainy morning in March in the early hours as she raced out the door for the coast, leaving her son in my care for the day. Kathie was working for a company installing business phones. She was at the beck and call of her employer to go anywhere in the region they serviced. Since Kathie was a single mom we were happy to step in to help wherever she needed. Her son, Andrew, often stayed with us while Kathie was working, and we loved it. He was a very special little guy and we all felt privileged to be able to care for him.

The ringing of the phone interrupted the quiet morning. The caller's voice saying Kathie was on her way to the hospital on the coast of Oregon shook me into action. They told me she had been found at the bottom of a steep embankment by some construction workers. She had been thrown from her car while driving to the early morning appointment. There had been lots of rain and a large slick area of pavement was the likely cause of the accident. Making arrangements for Andrew to stay with his other Grandma, Kathie's sister and I raced to the hospital.

We arrived mid-way through her 14-hour surgery to learn Kathie had suffered a head injury, internal injuries, compound fractures, and massive blood loss. The injuries seemed to be more than her petite body could bear.

As we stood in her room listening to the nurse report on the extent of the damage to our Kathie, it overwhelmed us beyond belief. We were told that due to the extreme nature of her injuries, the physicians were simply doing their best to put her back together and that they believed there was only a slim chance of survival.

Crisis of faith

It's funny how sometimes in moments of great distress, we seem to detach and step outside ourselves. As the nurse was speaking, something in me shifted. In the flash of a moment I saw that in

40

times of crisis, each of us has a choice. We can choose to be over-come by whatever obstacle presents itself and choose to be a victim of the circumstance or we can find the faith place that is there for us. Each response is influenced by a specific mindset. In this situation I had a choice to make. My family members had a choice. The nursing staff had a choice. The physicians had a choice.

We each would choose how we would respond to this crisis. This choice (and series of ongoing choices) would direct our actions from this point forward. It would also affect how and what we communicated with each other, not to mention how we would interact with Kathie. This communication would ultimately result in transmitting our belief to her … for her survival, for her outcome.

As I stood over her bed in ICU, I said to myself, "This person is my precious daughter. We know her as vibrant, outgoing, driven, focused, and fun. What we see with our eyes right now is not who she really is."

In the moment of this epiphany I could clearly see that the way we talked in front of her while she was unconscious could affect her survival. Her older sister Patsi and I determined that the nursing staff and all who interacted with her needed to start treating her like a person who would live rather than one who was dying. We made a choice and took action.

We placed her senior high school picture over her bed. This was the Kathie we knew. We wanted the staff to know her too. We allowed no negative conversations in the room. When we heard Kathie arouse enough to murmur her son's name over and over, "Andrew, Andrew, Andrew …," we went out and bought her a treasured Precious Moment's figurine of a mother and son at a gift store. Andrew looked so much like that blond-haired, blue-eyed boy in the figurine. We knew each time she

Choose how you respond to a crisis.

41

woke and saw it, it would remind her of another reason to fight for her life.

We placed that on her nightstand. I wanted it to be the first thing she saw when she woke to give her hope and purpose in her recovery. Her father, brothers, sister, and I kept vigil. Each of us wrestled with this crisis of faith in our own way.

Faith is a choice

I call this a crisis of faith because that is what it was. Faith believes in things that are unseen as though they are real. Our faith in the Creator of the Universe who is able to do miracles was juxtaposed with the contradiction we saw; the person we loved so dearly with injuries so severe that her survival was unlikely. We fought against the facts and data to believe in something that only could be seen in our faith … her full recovery. This was a moment by moment, day by day journey but in our faith, was the picture of her up and functioning again.

Miraculously, Kathie did recover. She still bears many scars in the parts of her body that almost didn't make it. She wore an external superstructure to provide traction for her bones for many months and the metal plates in her legs are still there to remind her of her miraculous survival.

It took many months in the hospital and intensive physical therapy and hard work over the years. It hasn't been easy for her. It certainly wasn't easy for us. Our family relationships were tested — some bonds were strengthened while others stretched to breaking.

This, one of the most challenging times of my life, taught me the cost of love.

Lessons learned

One of the costs of love is the faith in things hoped for but still unseen. I now fully understand how our faith (or belief in what is unseen as if it were real) is transmitted subconsciously through behaviors, words, and actions.

I discovered that when your faith is challenged, it forces you to choose. In a situation like this our faith was challenged over and over again providing many opportunities to practice how we would respond.

Seeing the results of this shift in thinking and how it affected Kathie's recovery made me think. I wondered, *What other areas of my life am I choosing a belief that actually creates a negative result? How could this change my relationships?*

I knew from experience that if I believed other than the best in someone I frequently got exactly what I believed in return and was discouraged with the outcomes. I decided to apply this new thinking — believing in others to create a positive result — to all my relationships. I was amazed at the positive outcomes! Of course, this was not an overnight transformation but over time, I consistently see that my belief in others impacts them as much as me.

An outrageous life is filled with rich relationships that cost ... that is the price of love.

An outrageous life is filled with rich relationships that cost. That is the price of love. We get to choose to believe. To have faith in what we do not see for the others in our life. For Kathie we believed in her recovery. For others I believe they are uniquely created by God and are able to accomplish great things, whatever those things are for them.

I'll be honest. It's not always an easy path. Life is hard and we all face difficulties but you are never a victim when you have faith operating in your life. Every day there are circumstances that will try to defeat you but it is your faith that helps you say, "This can work for good in my life."

Facing life's challenges with faith can take you to places where you will see goodness and grace you might not experience if your life is always champagne and roses.

There is a risk in being a person of faith ... but I would have it no other way!

The Bible is full of examples of people who had faith in hard times. The story of Moses leading his people through the Red Sea is one of my favorites. In their efforts to escape the pains and injustice of slavery, God led Moses and his people across the desert with the Egyptian army in hot pursuit. God's escape route included crossing the Red Sea as it parted to expose dry land. The faith of Moses and the people of Israel took them to that momentous event where they witnessed God's protection and power in a way they might had never known had they not taken the steps of faith that led them to that moment.

Our "Red Sea" experience was Kathie's recovery. It looked impossible, but through the experience we saw God's healing power in ways we would have never experienced in other day-to-day experiences. It took a crisis and our response of faith to experience the miracle.

Faith also brought me to the place where I could experience a miraculous emotional reunion with my family more than 20 years after Kathie's accident. I had faith that I could work to restore the wounded relationships but the full realization of that hope came during the Hawaii trip. I'll always be so thankful for that experience and the memories we created. I truly believe it came to be because of my choice to believe our relationships could be healed in spite of the struggles we faced.

There is a risk to being a person of faith. People sometimes think you are crazy or fanatical. You often are swimming upstream with your certainty that things will happen that contradict what seems to be happening around you. When you choose this path, you often are considered either a leader or a nut case. Either way, it's OK.

The principle of faith believes in what is unseen as if it were real. I love what trusting does for me. My relationships are built on trust and faith and I have good fruitful experiences to back that up. Relationships are richer because you can give without expectation of something in return. You can sow into others' lives and encourage them to be their best and watch them grow.

Faith keeps you hoping the best for them.

What about you?

Here are my questions for you:

1. How can you make the time you spend with friends and family count? What current relationships would benefit from switching your thinking to expect good things from these relationships? (i.e. work, family, friends, neighbors)

2. Describe a situation where you are having trouble believing in a positive outcome*.

3. Write out a positive belief you can adopt for this situation? What will reinforce that belief for you?

Hope, faith, and love are emotionally contagious. As carriers we physiologically transfer the energy of our belief. The cost of love in this situation is that we had to choose to believe despite the odds. It cost each of us personally but the rewards were many.

Love is patient, love is kind. It does not envy, it does not boast, it is not proud. It is not rude, it is not self-seeking, it is not easily angered, it keeps no record of wrongs. Love does not delight in evil but rejoices with the

*See our resources "Discerning Positive Character Traits in Negative Behavior"

truth. It always protects, always trusts, always hopes, always perseveres. And now these three remain: faith, hope and love. But the greatest of these is love (1 Corinthians 13: 4-7, 13).

From Kathie's Point of View:

It's funny how time works; how events from the distant past can feel like they happened yesterday. It doesn't seem that long ago I was lying in a hospital bed … staring at the ceiling tiles, brushing tears from my checks and wondering what would become of me and my young son. I had just been told I would most likely never walk again.

Devastating news at any age, I can still feel the remnants of emotion as I cycled between self pity, despair and anger. Why me?

The only future I could see was filled with hardship and handicap. At 23 years old, newly divorced with a 2-year-old son and all the baggage that brings, I could not imagine how I would survive this.

The recovery time in the hospital wasn't so bad during the day. When the sun was out and people were around it was much easier to put on the brave face. Those days seemed to go on forever. Doctors, nurses and therapists poking and prodding — they were a constant and ever present reminder of the reality of my broken body. The nights were the worst. The sadness was unbearable and my darkest fears seemed so real.

It was during those times I made late night phone calls to my father. He would listen to me cry out for assurance that everything would be OK. I know his heart must have been breaking for his little girl wishing he could take away my pain.

Have you ever wanted something so badly it hurts but you know the odds are against you? As this inevitable future began to reveal itself to me, somewhere in my broken body, my spirit cried out and I rebelled against what others said was my future. As a result, I learned a life changing truth: our destiny is shaped by what we choose to believe. As I lay in that hospital bed, this simple … or hard truth … comforted and compelled me.

I was the survivor of a single car accident. On my way to the coast, speeding along to get to an appointment on time, in the middle of nowhere I lost control of my car. No one knows what happened. I don't remember. As a matter of fact, as a result of the trauma, I lost a couple of weeks of memories.

I woke up to ask what happened and was only told my legs were broken. I would learn over time I had suffered a head injury, broken most of the bones from my ribs down and suffered massive internal injuries. My chances for survival were slim and the doctors actually told my family if I survived, I would never walk again. Weeks into my miracle recovery, I again faced the impossible as doctors advised amputation for my badly infected leg. Through the discouragement and fear, I realized I had a choice.

Even as the doctors and nurses told me again and again, not to get my hopes up, that I needed to prepare for a life of dependency and immobility, I refused to believe them. I know they meant well but I refused to believe that the picture they were painting of a life with wheelchairs and prosthetics was my future.

I was only 23. I had a life to live. I had a son to provide for. I had to believe I would walk again.

It was hard. The therapists would call me a baby and accuse me of not working hard enough. One doctor, who would call me overly optimistic, wrote in my medical records that I was refusing to face reality and in expecting a miracle, would be sorely disappointed. The pain and physical hardship was almost unbearable but I was determined to walk … and even dance again.

Grasping the inherent power of belief and taking responsibility for the choices I've made has helped me get through some pretty hard stuff. It has also taken me on a journey that has exceeded my wildest dreams.

In my hospital bed, I had a choice. I could choose to believe the physicians, lay back and accept my fate which would have been the easy route, or choose to fight, to work hard, and prove what I believed in my heart was true.

What does that look like in everyday life? Here is how it plays out. We are where we are today as a result of the choices we've made up to this point. Good or bad, right or wrong, we made those choices based on a set of beliefs. At any point in time we have an opportunity to adjust our course. If we want something different we have to make different choices.

(More of Kathie's story in Chapter 9)

Note about Kathie: Not only the co-author of this book, she is a successful speaker, business strategist, as well as a wife and mom to two adult sons, Andrew and Cameron.

While the accident 25 years ago left her with a permanent limp and residual pain, you wouldn't notice much since she is one determined woman. She takes the learning from this period in her life and uses it to influence others to bring their brilliance to the world and overcome any obstacles that might derail them.

Chapter Four

Leadership: Watering the Seeds of Greatness

How many times have you thought to yourself, "Someone should really be doing something about that?" That could mean anything from childhood hunger to the plight of the homeless to keeping the coffee in stock in the break room or streamlining the queue at the unemployment office.

> Leaders are born when people discover their gift and find their place.

Maybe you were the one who noticed something needed to be done to make another's life better in some small way. You may not have been the one to actually implement the change but you had the insight and heart to feel the need. This is where the seed of leadership starts.

I heard a sermon once where it was said that leaders are born when people discover their gift and find their place.

When you connect with your place, your gift comes alive. I've noticed early forms of leadership emerge with simple observations and the tugging of the heart toward an underserved people group. This could be in your own community or across the world; you might be helping someone in your office or someone you'll never meet. It usually happens like this — your natural desire to give or strength is triggered when you see a need. Your brain kicks in with a solution and tugs at your heart strings. Sometimes this is a gentle tug, other times it's a big pull that kicks you into action.

The tug began for me when I was touched through the books I read about the Holocaust. My heart was broken and compassion stirred inside me toward the Jews of the world, specifically in Israel. The heaviness on my heart only deepened as I gained more understanding from the Bible of God's view of the Jewish people and their place in the history and future of the world.

Up to this point in time, I really didn't know much about Israel at all. The more my interest grew, the more compelled I became to find an outlet to express it. This curiosity wouldn't seem to leave me alone. Employed full time, I had been searching for an opportunity to contribute to something that made a difference beyond just boosting my company's bottom line. This love and compassion for the Jews in Israel became a passion inside of me that would not be put away.

Your natural gifting or strength is triggered when you see a need.

When the door opened for me to visit Israel for the first time with a tour in 1984, I was looking for opportunities to serve. My excitement was hard to contain when I learned that the International Christian Embassy Jerusalem (ICEJ) was looking for a representative in the United State to bring awareness of the plight of the Jews in Russia, the "Refusniks."

I remember saying to myself, "WOW! This job sounds like it was designed for me."

Excited, I applied immediately and sat back to wait. And wait. I was sure the offer of a position with this organization would come any minute … yet no response.

Timing is everything

In the meantime, I started a full-time job traveling around the country for a company launching retirement facilities. While this position wasn't in any way my dream job of working with the people of Israel, it was shaping and refining my gifts. My time in this environment launched me into rich learning. The more I got involved with big picture management, team building, and coordination, my confidence grew.

Imagine my surprise when nine years later I learned the ICEJ was presenting a program at a local church near Charlotte, NC, where I lived at that time. Inside I was jumping up and down! I said to myself, "This could be it!"

As I got acquainted with the new leadership, I worked up the nerve to ask what had happened to the application I submitted nine years earlier. Unbeknownst to me, their leadership change had created a gap in their intake process. My application had fallen through the cracks during the transition. Whew! At least it wasn't about me.

When I re-applied to the new leadership for a volunteer job, the process went quickly and smoothly. Many leaders recommended me because I had built a reputation and proven myself over the years. I had to pinch myself … nine years earlier I had no skills in the area where they had need and I was an unproven person. Now they could see I was responsible and had continued to support Israel in all the ways I could find.

It was the beginning of many important years of serving in leadership for organizations that greatly utilized the skills and gifts that

God gave me. I had the seed of a vision. The timing had to be right for it to grow and produce fruit.

Leaders lead

The world needs leaders. You may be saying to yourself, "That's not me. I'm not a leader."

My response is, "Yes you are."

We can all choose to be leaders regardless of background, education, personality style, or anything else. More than standing up front with the bullhorn, or being the one in charge, leading has to do with seeing a need, feeling it in your heart, and taking a step to make a change.

Sometimes you'll do this by partnering with someone who is already in motion working to solve that problem or, it might be an issue where you are the one who leads the charge. Someone needs your gift, and you must serve it to the world

The stirring in my heart in 1984 led me to the opportunity nine years later to serve the ICEJ as a representative for Israel in this country. It was a thrilling time of blessing to work with teams from Israel and churches all over the U.S. I've been able to participate in bringing artists and musicians from Israel to perform and teach our local communities their traditional dances and songs. It was an incredible time with the ICEJ.

A few years later, both my daughter Patsi and I were coordinating and taking groups from the U.S. to Israel so they could build relationships within the communities they were praying for.

It is an interesting side note that during this period I was struggling financially. Wanting desperately to give and lacking the resources is a challenging place to be. The tension of that mental space can be very stressful. I am sure you know what I am talking about. When we are trying to make ends meet it is easy to say to yourself, "Let someone else contribute who has more money, more time, and more talent."

If you have the tug on your heart for any group or person, don't ignore it. Your ability to see and feel the need is calling you to lead. Just get in and start even if it is small or feels insignificant. If not you, then who?

Lessons learned

Even in the midst of my own financial difficulty, I saw God provide in amazing ways. There were days I couldn't afford food. By divine coincidence, on those days my landlord would call down the stairs to me to offer some of the food that was left over from their restaurant. There was no way they could have known my need. This strengthened my faith and focus.

What are divine coincidences other than God showing you that He loves you and is caring for your needs?

The more I saw His provision for me, the more I wanted to stretch my belief and understanding for others. I used my passion for this cause to set my financial goals over the last 25 years knowing that whatever income opportunities I chose to pursue I needed to leverage them so I could give more to support Israel. I now am able to help widows, orphans, Holocaust survivors and Christian Ministries like ICEJ who help both Jews and Arabs. I am truly filled full for that privilege in my life.

When I follow the thread from the first tug on my heartstrings to the affect on the people and communities years later, I am reminded of a couple of things.

- I never saw myself as having world impact. I only knew I felt a compassion for this group of people.

- I couldn't rush the process. Every step toward contribution opened new doors.

- My gift mix is continually being refined as I step out and follow my heart.

Here are my questions for you:

1. What need have you seen in your community that you wish someone would do something about?

2. Is there something you can do to make that happen? If so, what can you do?

3. What keeps you from following through on your impulse to contribute?

Bette's challenge

Leadership and contribution are so closely intertwined. Our world needs more of us to step up and take responsibility. Is this your time? Is that nudge in your heart your wakeup call?

You are uniquely positioned at this place and time to do what you can do. Whatever that is. Will you step out of your own "busyness" and lead where you are?

Here are just a few suggestions of areas in your community where you can serve:

- schools/education: volunteering to read with young students, tutor, help at-risk kids

- community/neighborhood enrichment: cleaning parks

- the arts: volunteer to help with community music, theater, arts programs

- at risk groups such as the elderly, single parents, poor, homeless, etc.

- Disaster/crisis relief: prepare emergency kits for organizations

- Refugee assistance (many communities have large refugee populations who need help with finding resources, physicians, housing, help registering their children for school, etc.)

- Healthcare — volunteering at hospitals, nursing homes, hospice centers, etc.

- Foster Care

- Mentoring through Big Brother/Big Sister Programs

True fulfillment comes from giving and making your life count.

Chapter Five

The Power of Contribution

I'll never forget the first time I read a book on the Holocaust. I was totally shocked as I read *The Diary of Anne Frank* and Corrie Ten Boom's *The Hiding Place*, accounting their experiences during this time in history. Each time I read a new book sharing accounts of suffering and injustice during the Holocaust, I wept my way from page to page as I learned about the horrific things that had happened to the Jews simply because they were Jews.

In my late 30s I was still new to the Christian faith. I was just learning about the history of that faith and things that God cared about. I knew that Jews were called "God's chosen people" and they were always on His heart.

You can be the change you want to see in the world!

No person or group of people ever deserved to be treated the way they were. I couldn't wrap my mind around an evil that would send a family in an airless box car to face abuse, starvation, and certain extermination. The injustice was beyond my comprehension.

Even now, years later, I still am overwhelmed with the unspeakable atrocities. I know the Jews were not the only victims of the Holocaust but it just happened that was where I started to learn. I still watch movies about the Holocaust when they come into my hands (most recently *The Boy In The Striped Pajamas*) because I don't want to forget and become desensitized to this example of man's inhumanity to man.

On my visits to Israel, I go through Yad Vashem and the Children's Memorial hall where it names all the children who perished in the Holocaust. There is a light lit for each child in that hall. The bravery in times of great fear, the faith in times of horror, and the love shown through acts of profound sacrifice are clearly visible as I read through my tears.

Books like these find their way into my hands over and over again. They have forever changed me. The more I read and learned about this group of people, a nagging urge was planted in my heart. I wanted to do something for those who carry personal memories and the mark of this horrendous history even after 50 years. While I knew I could pray and encourage the ones I met, I dreamed of doing more.

What could I do? I was just a stay-at-home mom.

But what could I do? I was just a stay-at-home mom.

I had been married nearly 20 years at this point with kids spread out in their teen years. A variety of activities from school plays, sports, dance lessons, and more kept us very busy. I was wrapped up in a life a world away from those I prayed for. Little did I know how a small nation a half a world away would change my life forever.

Prior to becoming aware of the atrocities the Jews had endured I didn't really even know anyone who was Jewish. But as I studied and learned more about the people and the culture, I was actually drawn to their communities everywhere I turned. In social groups, professional groups and even casual acquaintances the subject of the Holocaust and Jewish traditions would surface. Even those who had become "hidden" due to their intermarriage with non-Jews would surface with their stories.

For many years I was aware of the continuing struggle the Jews faced around the world with anti-Semitism and political control of their country, but didn't have the slightest interest in traveling to Israel. I was sure it was too dangerous and couldn't even imagine myself in a place like that.

One day, suddenly, my heart changed! I found myself considering what it would be like to visit, where I would go, who I would go with and how I would get myself there. I just had a "knowing" it was time to go. I was more surprised than anyone. (God does things like that sometimes).

I began a quiet investigation to follow this urging in my heart. I discovered that a Christian Group I had heard of before was going for The Feast of Tabernacles[3] and it was about a month away. Still every circumstance told me it was impossible for me to go.

I still had kids living at home and no money for a trip like that and it seemed like a preposterous idea to even suggest that I do such a far out thing. However, I had no idea things would change and my circumstances would be different, almost overnight.

I had read about the Feast of Tabernacles[4] in the Bible but was clueless about its current significance. All I knew was what I heard in my heart. As I began to inquire, I discovered that every fall the International Christian Embassy in Jerusalem hosted the Feast for Christians all over the world.

What seemed so impossible came together quickly. I simply sold my computer for just the amount I needed for the trip. By divine coincidence, someone was right there ready to buy it. I made my reservation and I was on my way! I was able to travel with the

[3] The ICEJ holds the Feast for Christians every fall.
[4] Feast of Tabernacles reference (Lev. 23:33-43)

group I had contacted and we were there for three full weeks. All this happened just one month after I felt the initial prompting to go to Israel. Amazing! There I was! In the Land of Israel!

I was amazed to see how God opened the door for me to be in Israel for this Biblical celebration. The Feast of Tabernacles is the Festival of Ingathering of the last harvest for the year. It is a Feast of Joy. It is a great time to be in the City of The Great King. I highly recommend this time for your first visit.

> Core values drive everything, and when you tap into your core values, you can significantly impact your world!

As the departure date approached, my enthusiasm couldn't totally dispel the fear of traveling to a country where people were always fighting. I could hear the chatter in my mind, *It can't be a safe place for travel. Are you putting yourself in harm's way? What about your family?*

What a misrepresentation that turned out to be. From the moment I stepped off the plane onto the tarmac at Ben Gurion airport, I was in love. Instead of feeling like a visitor, I felt like I was coming home. I felt a deep heart connection to the land and people. The fears for my safety quickly disappeared as I learned Israel is a place that is very special. I never had a sense for a moment that I was in danger or anything was a threat.

Going up to Jerusalem

The land is beautiful and plants and trees bloom everywhere. As we drove up to Jerusalem, it took my breath away. It truly is an amazing "City on a Hill." It is a wonderful blend of the old and the new.

We went straight to the Western Wall for prayer before we even went to our hotel. It was 11 p.m., but was an incredible way to start a visit in the Land. We were greatly touched by the sense of history and God's presence in that place.

In the Old Walled City, the cars and donkeys were side by side on the narrow streets. The divisions of the Old City revealed different cultures thriving in the same small area. Inside our tour bus we could hear the sounds of church bells and the muezzins at the mosques calling the Muslims for prayer echoing the contrasts of this great city.

During that first trip, I could see an opportunity for contribution as I asked the question that was still weighing on my mind, *What can I do to make a difference?*

I began to get an idea of how I could encourage and support Israel and the Jewish people. The first thing I noticed was how Israel's economy depends heavily on tourism. When there is fear to travel it really hurts the country's economy. I observed Christians and faith-based communities from all over the world travel to Israel to experience the Biblical sites and culture.

They, in particular, are excited to experience history and stand ready to invest in that pilgrimage. This Feast of Tabernacles was no different. Seventy nations were represented at the Feast that year with over 5,000 people attending. This particular event attracts the largest group of tourists to travel to Israel in the whole year. I could organize tours and bring people over to experience this just like I had. Soon that was a reality.

Follow your heart. It will lead you to opportunites that make up some of the richest elements of your life!

During this trip, we participated in a march to honor Israel where we carried banners with Biblical promises encouraging Israel. Thousands of Christians, many dressed in native costumes, walked in pouring rain for several miles demonstrating their support. Our intent was to communicate our understanding to the people of this land that we felt God was with them.

The Feast itself was a wonderful experience for me. The colors and the music were amazing and all the dancing … well, I was ready to stay longer. The vibrancy of the culture and the people I had read about for so long captured my heart. I knew I would feel a connection with this land and its people long after I boarded the plane to go home.

After returning home from that first trip, I began to see what I could do to help in the area of encouraging tourism. My first step in contributing to this country and people was to plan on organizing tours for the different Biblical celebrations such as the Feast of Tabernacles.

Soon I was bringing back pastors and Christian leaders and teaching them how to organize tours for their churches and groups. We arranged the tours to immerse visitors in the local culture by arranging visits and meals with local families and many exciting connections occurred. The result of this cultural exchange was significant. Several people who took the original tours maintain friendships with those Israeli families even today.

Find something on the outer edges of your comfort zone that also helps other people … and do it!

Our new Jewish friends appreciated our support, but on one of my early trips there was a comment from a host in the settlement community that I'll never forget. We were in the part of the country the world calls "The West Bank" but is actually Biblical Israel. He said, "Bette, I had no idea there were people who cared about us outside of our own country!"

As he recounted condemning stories heard on western media outlets and on local news, I began to understand how isolated they felt. The more I questioned, the more I understood the effect of the isolation and the difficult living situations of those living in the settlement communities. This challenged and inspired me to figure out what more I could do to contribute.

Discover what breaks your heart

It became clear at this time in my life that learning more about the State of Israel and the Jewish people struck a deep chord inside me. At the time I had no idea that this had to do with my own core values, specifically the value I hold about people who are underserved or mistreated. What I know now is that our core values drive our actions and responses and when tapped, they can move us to impact our world in significant ways.

What about you?

> Are you currently involved in contributing to something outside your own sphere?

> Are you motivated to contribute by something that wrenches your gut?

I will be honest, I had volunteered for other organizations before getting involved with Israel but none of the causes touched my heart as deeply as this.

Follow your values until you discover what breaks your heart. This is your key to changing the world. This first venture pursuing significant contribution led to many opportunities over the next several years. I continue to contribute in The Land nearly 40 years later. I have a deep love for the Jews and have found them to be a passionate and compassionate people.

Lessons learned

Contribution connects a person to opportunities, not only personally but professionally.

Through pursuing this interest I gained outrageous opportunities for a person of my limited background.

Nearly 10 years after my first trip, I was privileged to work with the International Christian Embassy in Jerusalem. Later I became the Executive Director of a Colorado-based ministry. We connected settlements in Israel with Christian churches in the U.S. who wanted to support them in prayer, letter writing and fund raising to help build playgrounds in the Settlement communities. I've spoken in churches and communities across the U.S., sharing the story of the settlements on the West Bank and their plight.

> **Your core values drive your actions, and when tapped, they can move you to impact the world!**

I grew personally and spiritually as I learned and participated in the Biblical feasts and celebrations with those who'd been keeping the tradition for centuries. Watching and participating in the lives of those who are still living the Biblical traditions helped me understand I could enjoy those traditions too. It has given me a true love for the Torah, which is how the Jews refer to the Hebrew Scriptures or the Old Testament.

Following those first stirrings of my heart to get involved led to many other opportunities to meet the needs of people in that area of the world. I met people I would have never met, I had adventures I would have never experienced, and I took risks — all on behalf of a people whose alienation and mistreatment over a significant period in our history compelled me to reach out.

What about you?

Here are my questions for you:

1. What social causes break your heart?

2. What talents can you contribute to that cause?

3. What is a first step you can take to contribute to a cause you care about?

I supported the cause that was on my heart at that time in any way I could. I kept doing so throughout many times of challenge and transition. It stretched me personally to follow my heart and led me to the opportunities that make up some of the richest elements of my life today.

My question for you is, "What are you waiting for?"

Step out and change your world!

> "Only those who have learned the power of sincere and selfless contribution experience life's deepest joy: true fulfillment." — *Anthony Robbins*

I want what she's got

Chapter Six

Surviving Contradiction

Living an outrageous life isn't always smooth sailing. Those who make choices to live an outrageous life often face challenges and obstacles along the way.

Let's be honest — sometimes life is hard and we face tough times. An outrageous life can give us some of the tools to face these problems head on rather than cower in a corner waiting for the storms to pass.

To experience the incredible highs, sometimes you have to go through some very dark, lonely places. Many times life can feel like a roller coaster you will never get off ... until you break through to find the internal stabilizer available to you any time, especially in the challenges.

Some of the most intense personal growth (in other words ... *best* and *worst* times of my life) occurred in the years after my divorce. I was living on the East Coast, far from my children and friends, starting a new life. But the reality of starting over isn't always the glamorous idea you envision. You never think certain things are going to happen to you ... like having no food, having no money, or sleeping in your car. Those things happen to other people. That's what I thought. My fresh start definitely had its challenges.

Some say, "When the going gets tough, the tough get going." I didn't feel so tough, but I had to keep going. En route from west to east, I providentially came across the Stephen Covey seminars. Covey made me aware of my personal mission statement, which gave me the focus I desperately needed during this transition. I became certified in the DiSC Behavioral assessment programs, which opened the door for new career possibilities.

> To experience the incredible hights, sometimes you have to go through some very dark, lonely places.

Shortly after my company relocated me to Montgomery, Alabama, they decided to eliminate my position. They immediately came to pick up all the rental furniture they had provided, even though I wasn't moving until the end of the month. I knew I'd be limited to what I could carry in my car wherever I decided to move, so I went out and bought a small computer, card table, and chair. Since I had no furniture except for what I'd just purchased, a big lambskin became my mattress and I slept on the floor.

During those weeks I went to classes for Covey and the DiSC training. I prayerfully waited for direction. I needed to know where to go from there. I decided to check out the Charlotte area, which was three to four hours from Montgomery. I didn't know anyone in either city and had limited finances to rent. I was afraid to live alone in a strange town, but I went … and stayed in a hotel my first few nights. My first task was to find a place to live. Providentially, I only looked in one area and found a Christian family with a basement apartment to rent on a beautiful lake. It was to be another journey of faith.

There I was, sitting at a card table with a new computer teaching myself technology at the age of 55. I remember the battle between the voices in my head. One said with a sneer, "Are you crazy? Do you really think you can pull this off?" and the other cheered me on with, "You can do anything you put your mind to. Your faith in God has brought you this far. He is not going to leave you hanging."

Listening to the Covey and DiSC training tapes in my car as I traveled not only led me to a deeper understanding of myself, but opened my eyes to patterns of behavior from my past relationships. I shook my head at some of the insights revealed through the tapes, thinking to myself, "If I'd only known, things could have been so different."

What a contradiction! Here I was, stranded in an emotional desert, disconnected from my family, struggling professionally, and trying to start my life over with very few resources with a greater understanding of how I got here but no means to do anything about it. Could things get any worse?

When I finally settled outside of Charlotte, NC, I left for work every day consumed with the stress of having no money and scraping by to eek out this new life. And yet, even at my lowest, I was surrounded by God's natural beauty. The view from my daylight basement apartment overlooked Lake Wylie in North Carolina. It was a community framed by lovely sprawling trees and homes tucked in around the lake. It was during this time I launched my own corporate training and personal development company with my new tools in hand. I was bootstrapping every step of the way.

Surprised by generosity

Making ends meet was tiring, but I slugged on. The outrageous part of my life at this time had nothing to do with my ability to bring in income and resources but in the way I was blessed by generosity from others. The owners of the apartment I was renting lived above me. They often shared leftovers from the slower days at the restaurant and these meals helped me survive between paychecks. Along with providing food, the invitations to join them on boating trips around the lake every weekend fed my body and my soul.

It gets hot in North Carolina in the summer. If you've ever experienced "cloying" heat … this was it. Trying to stretch every dime and save on gas expenses, I made the decision not to use my car air conditioner. Driving to appointments that were a couple of hours away I would arrive hot and more than just a little rumpled. How I got business in those days can only be attributed to God's grace to me. Through tears I would pray, "God, thank you for training me. Thank you for providing." I always asked for grace while He trained me for the future. He knew what I needed even when I didn't.

Hold on to God's promises!

Early in my new business venture, I needed to make a business trip that required an overnight stay. With no money for a hotel room, sleeping in my car seemed like the only option. As I was preparing to leave, the phone rang. It was my good friend Gretchen. After a few pleasantries, I told her about my travel plans. I was amazed when she said, "Bette, if you are going to be in Columbia, SC, you need to stay with my friend." Gretchen didn't know my plans to sleep in my car, but God certainly did. It was yet another amazing provision reminding me that He was looking out for me.

This period of my life was very desperate. In my own limited experience and view point, I could only see hard work and lonely times ahead … except for the belief I had in something bigger than me.

The stress really got to me at times, and once, while on an important appointment, I discovered that I had on shoes that were the same style but two different colors! I hurriedly ran from the appointment and when I got home, threw the shoes into my closet and cried hot tears of frustration and shame.

In spite of these struggles, I held on to God's promise, *"I will make all things work together for good for those who love Me and are called according to My purpose"* (Romans 8:28). There was no doubt in my mind that much of what I was facing was the result of choices I had made.

And yet, I also knew this time was preparing me for something more. I wasn't quite sure how to make different choices yet, but I was learning that I was responsible. I had faith that God keeps His word. I believed that what He says is true.

Faced with the contradiction of what I was currently experiencing and what I believed my future might hold, I refused to give up hope.

Lessons learned

Life gives us all many peaks and valley experiences, with highs and lows and contradictions in between. Learning to respond *rather than react* to circumstances is one of the keys to enjoying the truly outrageous life. I've bottomed out more times than I'd care to count. The brutal truth about hitting "bottom" (whatever the bottom is for you) is that there really is nowhere to go but up. On your way up (or down), you can choose how you respond.

> On your way up (or down), you can choose how you respond.

Understanding the power of your choice … this is the stabilizer. When I realized I could only control myself and my responses, not my circumstances, I gained control. The challenge of living in the contradiction is that so many things appear out of your control. Combine the power of your choice with the power of faith (faith is defined as *"being sure of what we hope for and certain of what we do not see"* Hebrews 11:1) and you have a surefire combination for truly outrageous living.

Assess the gap between where you are and where you want to be. One way to do this is by completing the assessment tool in Chapter 9. The questions will help you discover some of the challenges you might be facing in living an outrageous life. I encourage you to take time to reflect and look for ways to practice positive responses to the challenges in your life. This kind of attitude can help you move closer to the outrageous life you deserve.

What about you?

Here are my questions for you:

1. Draw a horizontal line on a page. At one side, use a few words to describe where you are in your life. At the opposite end, use a few words to describe where you want to be. Assess the gap from where you are to where you want to be. Where are you in the contradiction?

2. What behaviors, attitudes, or misconceptions are getting in your way?

3. How can you move closer to where you want to be? What can you invest in that will help move you forward?

I discovered more about myself in the valleys of life than in the peaks. Hardship can be the growing place for our character and help us discover character qualities we didn't know we had.

You have to break the cycle of limitations to get where you want to go.

You must identify the problems in your way. You can get feedback from friends and from people who care about you to help you get unstuck. Noted speaker and author Brian Klemmer says, "Feedback is the breakfast of champions. It is the information from which you can make corrections, be more effective and make timely changes" (*When Good Intentions Run Smack into Reality*, p.67).

A coach, mentor, or accountability partner can help you see blind spots and give you helpful feedback.

Sometimes we have to break the cycle of limitations we have put on ourselves to get where we want to go. Put yourself in a place of new growth, finding new solutions to replace the old ways of doing things and challenge you to be more. This can be one of your first steps to a truly outrageous life!

I want what she's got

I want what she's got

Chapter Seven

Living a Healthy, Outrageous Life

If you had met me in 2002, you might have thought, "That woman is acting like she's in a fog!" And you'd have been right! I felt like I was in a fog … I was experiencing gaps in memory and a serious loss of mental clarity. It was getting hard to connect my thoughts with my words!

I didn't realize it at the time but I was in a serious (for me) health crisis. For years it was my family first. After they were grown and my divorce left me out on my own, my health wasn't really a priority. Earning a living and staying afloat was first and foremost in my mind. Taking care of my body was pretty far down my list of priorities.

I was always busy and as long as I could keep going, I did. I didn't know I had a problem until I was stopped in my tracks with the realization that my health was suffering and there was something really wrong. The sad thing was I knew better. A traumatic experience years earlier had shown me the importance of taking care of my health. I had forgotten this valuable lesson and was paying for my poor choices. It was time to take action to make sure my health would allow me to live the life of purpose I had recently rediscovered.

The call that changed my life

After my husband Floyd retired from the Navy, we settled in a small town in Southern Oregon. I was in my 40s and enjoying the stage of life of having older kids — still needing me but gaining independence. Though I was struggling in my marriage, one of the bright spots in this time of my life was having my parents move to the area. They built a house just about a mile from ours to be closer to their grandchildren and me.

My parents were retired and they loved to travel. They were in great shape and in addition to their own travels; they vacationed with us for several years. Their trips kept them busy and made living close a great blessing instead of a hardship. They had their own lives but when they were home, they were active participants in our family. Our home was the gathering place. This period of time, with my family around me, seemed to be the picture of what every young woman wants.

Start with prayer, arm yourself with knowledge, and then take action.

In the summer of 1972, my parents were in Santa Barbara enjoying a sunny California getaway. Not expecting them back for a few days, I was surprised to get a phone call out of the blue from my dad. The call rocked my world and changed my ideas about health care forever.

The voice on the phone trembled as he said to me, "Honey, I'm paralyzed. I've just been diagnosed with Hodgkin's lymphoma. The cancer has wrapped around my spinal cord." My hands began to shake as I grasped the phone and tears came to my eyes as he said, "Please pray with me!" He was scared. So was I.

My parents had been having a typical vacation, enjoying outdoor activities, dining out and living the carefree life of retirees. My dad had experienced some back pain, but thought nothing of it and they continued with their vacation. One sunny morning he woke thinking he'd be enjoying another day of sightseeing and browsing through the local shops with my mom. As he tried to get up, he realized he couldn't move. The panic struck quickly as he realized he was paralyzed. A call for help, a trip to the hospital and some anxious waiting yielded a surprising diagnosis — cancer.

The power of knowledge

Cancer is a scary word. Back in the 1970s, the word itself caused fear and uncertainty, shadowed by suffering and death. I had a few friends who had faced this in their own lives, but I didn't know much about the true nature of the disease. Searching for something to do and wanting to help my dad in a practical way, I started to learn everything I could about cancer treatments. I was thrown into life's school of learning and found there was a lot to know.

Back in those days, the typical treatment was chemotherapy and radiation. As word of my dad's diagnosis began to spread among his friends, we learned of a family who had successfully treated cancer with some alternative therapies. Hearing this family's story changed my focus. Instead of only researching traditional treatments, I began to look at alternative therapies. This shift changed how I approached the issues of health and wellness in my family.

Bringing home stacks of books from the library and making frequent visits to health food stores (they weren't easy to find in the 70s!), I began to read everything I could get my hands on about alternative medicine. My dad did have surgery to free his spinal cord and after talking with his friends who experienced success with alternative medicine, he decided to head for Mexico for some treatments. They were successful and got him back on his feet quickly. He began the health and nutrition routine they suggested and in no time he was on the golf course and traveling back and forth from Oregon to Mexico where he loved to fish.

The results spoke for themselves. Alternative medicine had given my dad a second chance. What I learned empowered me and I began to take an even greater interest in my family's health. I integrated much of what I had learned in my research into our diet and health practices at home.

You need to be paying attention to what goes into your body.

My family had been gardening for years to save money feeding our large family, but now I realized the value of having fresh vegetables in our diet and began canning and preserving as much as I could, not just because my husband mandated it, but because I knew it would improve the health of my children. I even introduced healthy ideas like making fresh bread from ground wheat and sprouts every week.

Looking into alternative options and questioning what is taken as commonly accepted medical practice became a way of life. It was a matter of life or death for my dad. I would no longer just take a physician's diagnosis or treatment plan just because it was said by a health professional. I now knew there were other ideas, options and practices that could influence health and well being that fell outside of the traditions of western medicine.

For several years my dad continued to live a normal life while continuing to take the supplements he received in Mexico. On one of his visits home he went back to his doctor in Oregon for a check-up. Even though dad was feeling fine, the doctor suggested a preventative round of chemotherapy to ensure the cancer wouldn't return.

What happened is both tragic and telling. Dad's immune system was compromised as a result of the chemotherapy. With a weakened immune system, he caught pneumonia and complications from this illness took his life. Our family was wracked with grief. How could this happen? He was doing so well.

My dad was only 68 years old when he died. There was little gratification that the autopsy report showed no sign of Hodgkin's lymphoma or any cancer at all. While I know there is place for traditional medicine and chemotherapy can be a vital tool in treating some forms of cancer, for my dad, it was the wrong call.

Becoming my own advocate

This health awareness stuck with me. From that point on, I knew I needed to be paying attention to what I put in my body and become as active as I could in my own health care. Years later when a doctor recommended I have a hysterectomy, I did some research and realized I could alleviate some of my symptoms with physical therapy. I found a solution that didn't require surgery. I continued to advocate for my family's health and intended to take care of myself too.

As driven as I was after I was out on my own, it shouldn't have been a big surprise when, as I reached 60, I found myself having some issues. This state of having a mental fog that I just couldn't shake was more than just being tired or worn out. This cloudy confusion had me struggling to carry on conversations. It was like my words were spelled out on a Scrabble board and someone kept shaking the pieces so they no longer made any sense.

This loss of mental clarity had crept up over time. I lived by myself, was focused on my career, and kept pretty busy. I shrugged off the periodic occasion where I couldn't find the words to complete my thought or couldn't get focused but when it became more frequent I began to get scared. The implications to my work, for my family, for my life, became almost more than I could bear.

I tried to hide this with laughter and jokes, blaming my gaps in understanding and focus on "senior moments." But it was more than that. I started to worry that my future might be in jeopardy if I couldn't work. My kids started to guess something was wrong with me and suspected that I might be experiencing the early onset of Alzheimer's.

I had to come to grips with the fact that I had a problem and that it had to be addressed. Something had to change. Turns out I had a few things to change ... the way I ate, my schedule, and my stress level.

In 1997, researchers at UCLA began to investigate the nutritional drop in food value based on samples from 1953. What they discovered was that the fresh foods grown today have significantly less nutritional value than 50 years ago due to the nutrient depleted soil. My body was not getting what it needed for optimum brain function. I might have written off my symptoms to the aging process but because I learned to ask questions about my health I was able to find real solutions to my problems. As I began asking my friends about how they felt and what they did to support their health I learned about supplements that support brain function and reduce the impact of toxins (all the chemicals, pesticides, and preservatives) that build up in our bodies over time.

When a friend suggested I try a simple cleansing and nutritional program it immediately helped. My brain fog, low energy, and sleepless nights disappeared within days. I continue with the program eight years later and I have changed my lifestyle to include better nutrition, detoxing (flushing out new toxins as they come in) and I have incorporated a schedule that includes rest, exercise, and less stress so I can build a life that will keep me healthy as long as I live.

A new, healthy, outrageous life!

All the work I had done to begin a new life after my divorce was worthless if I didn't have the health to enjoy it. My Dad's health crisis had shown me that advocating for my own health was so important it could mean the difference between life and death. Since starting my new health practices, I've been able to live a truly outrageous life! I have the energy I need to have a successful career (even at age 73!) and the energy to spend quality time with family and friends doing the things I love.

I thought I was experiencing the early onset of Alzheimers!

During certain phases of our lives — raising children, working, maintaining marriages and other significant relationships — it's easy to lose sight of our own self-care. Our health is one of those areas that reflect how closely we pay attention to ourselves. Our emotional and physical well-being contributes to or detracts from the outrageous life experience.

Doing nothing is a choice that leaves you the victim! There's no time like the present to take care of you. The times in my life where I've felt the most engaged, positive, and empowered were those where I felt in control of my choices.

I encourage you to decide today to take charge of your health. You can start small — change one bad habit to one good one this month. Then pick another one for next month. Investigate what keeps you from fully engaging with the life you want. Taking care of myself was an important step that moved me toward the outrageous life I experience today. The funny thing is I thought I was managing this pretty well when the mental fog showed me otherwise. I learned that my outlook, my vision for the future, and my attitude were all influenced by my health.

What about you?

Here are my questions for you:

1. What is it about your health that restricts you? (i.e. energy, physical, mental, motivation)

81

2. What areas of your life suffer because you don't function at your optimum level? (i.e. family, career, recreation)

3. List two negative health habits you could replace with two positive ones? (i.e. diet, exercise, sleep, stress, water intake) What patterns of behavior will you need to change to accomplish this?"

Take time to invest in your health so you too can live outrageously!

"I pray that you may prosper in all things and be in health, just as your soul prospers" (3 John 1:2).

That sounds like an outrageous life to me!

Note: After personally experiencing success I chose to pursue a career with the company that manufactures the nutritional cleansing products that helped me get my energy back. I've found a career I love — helping people live a healthy, outrageous life! While many good nutritional programs exist, let's face it, it only takes some attention to what you put in your body to improve your overall health. I encourage you to take steps to research and learn how changes in diet, supplements, and toxins can affect your overall health. Look for reputable websites, organizations and resources that promote healthy habits and practices. (If you're curious, you can learn more about the products that helped me at my company's website, www.thepeoplebuilders.isagenix.com.)

Chapter Eight

A New Beginning

We wrestled the umbrella at the Grand Junction Starbucks into just the right position to protect us from the intense sun and settled into our chairs to enjoy the breeze that cooled the air. I sipped my Americano in the warm sunshine and sat amazed as three of my kids bantered deep in conversation connecting, encouraging, and strategizing ... a scene that most likely would not have taken place had it not been for the changes in my life over the last five years. I felt so privileged to see the ripple effects of my own personal transformation manifest in them. All this stemmed from my decision and choice to re-engage with life ... to live with purpose and intention rather than be a victim.

The story of my life has been less than the happily-ever-after tale I would like to have passed on to my children. A life of hurts, disappointments, and unmet expectations kept me from fully engaging and investing in the lives of those around me for many years, especially my kids. The consequences of poor choices I made early on in my life continue to reveal themselves. While some of the relationships in my life are on their way to restoration others are still broken — an ever-present pain to my heart.

If you are a parent, you understand this gut-wrenching love you have for your kids. When that connection is broken, it hurts to the core. One of the lessons I've learned is that it's never too late to invest in the lives of others ... especially your family.

You've heard the saying "what goes around comes around" to illustrate the universal principle of sowing and reaping. The idea that if you do good things you get good things back or, if you are careless or hurtful you can expect to be hurt in return, is timeless. I've found I can put the odds in my favor to sow and reap goodness if I practice seeking the good in others.

What goes around ... truly does come around.

Because of an unhappy marriage and struggles through my life, I was a very self-absorbed person. The pain and loneliness was a constant reminder that for some reason, I just wasn't measuring up — as a wife, mother, or daughter. I spun in circles trying to find ways to fix these problems, but they all centered on my needs, my desires, and my wants.

When I started living my life with purpose and intent, I made a conscious choice to try to be more "other-focused." When I decided to change the way I interacted in my relationships, I was amazed at how quickly those around me responded.

This may sound like a difficult step. It isn't. There is opportunity around you every day. Whether at the grocery store, with your family, or with your many service providers, you have opportunities to create positive impact. In the beginning, I took small steps. I hosted a discussion group where friends and acquaintances could meet in my home to discuss life values, challenges, and deepen relationships. The more I was involved in groups like this, the more I learned to serve others.

This generosity of spirit expanded from hospitality to consistently meeting with friends to encourage and pray for them and to participating in regular outreach in the community. This shift in my attitude and awareness was initiated over 40 years ago when I cried out for help and God heard me. When I was motivated by having my needs met first and foremost, I could not truly reach out and serve others. Because I was changed in the moment that God met me, I knew I was loved, accepted, and valued. As a result, I was no longer driven to meet my own needs first.

My recently-renewed purpose to leave a legacy and develop leaders who desire to make a difference in the world directs my energy to reach out to others. Regardless of the situation, I'm now looking for creative ways to contribute, build up, and serve others.

This doesn't mean I am on top of my game all the time. Like most, I have moments of serious doubt about my own ability to contribute. *What am I worth? Can I really make a difference? Am I fooling myself?*

It's at times like these when the power of encouraging words comes back around to remind me that the law of sowing and reaping proves true.

I had a major crisis of confidence not long ago. I was set off by a questionnaire asking me about my accomplishments. I don't feel sometimes like I've done much in my life, so my "gremlins" came out, leaving me to wrestle with my own doubts and beliefs for a few days. By divine appointment, a few days later I opened an email from a young man I'd recently reconnected with while in Southern California. I'd been close with his parents when my kids were in high school but we had lost touch over the years. I

Can you really make a difference? You absolutely can!

was delighted to spend an evening with him and my daughters, remembering past adventures and renewing friendship with this very special friend.

His email let me know how powerful our reconnection had been. Our meeting came at a time when he was facing deep discouragement and he shared how close to the edge he was at that time. Here is an excerpt from his message to me:

Dear Bette,

I have been thinking about you for quite some time. I want to fill you in and tell you how God has blessed me through you. First of all, when I met you for dinner, I was very closed off to God. I can't think of anyone else in the world that could have gotten through to me except you and your family.

I must also tell you that when I was living with my parents in Oregon last winter, I was trying to grasp what a Christian should look like. I decided that it looked just like you in how you bless everyone with your resources and love. I wondered what I could do with my little means and decided one day to buy not only my coffee at Starbucks, but for the several people behind me. What happened is that people started doing the same thing and it snowballed. It ended up blessing everyone, including the staff, as nobody had to purchase their own coffee for most of that day. I made this a daily habit, as it was a simple yet effective way of showing God's love in action; I was just doing what you do on a small scale.

This idea made it to the Dream Centre on the Gold Coast in Australia through friend of mine, and their pastor ran with it. He calls it their ARK Program (Acts of Random Kindness). He asks his 1000 members to do at least 10 ARKs per week, which is 40 thousand per month. The ARK program has changed the whole culture of their church and is getting lots of positive attention from the community. They call themselves "Arkoholics" because they are addicted to helping others — just like YOU!

Now other Christian denominations in the community want to be part of it, so they are trying to raise money to build a huge ARK Community Center to bring all the denominations under one roof to celebrate God's love in action. They are even getting support from the local government because it is doing so much good for the people in the community.

What is even more amazing, Bette, is that God gave me the name "ARK" clear back in January in a very powerful spiritual vision. It was placed so heavy on my heart that I saw everything in detail. I knew this was my future. This is the only time this has ever happened to me and I can't tell you how powerful it was. Every detail of the ARK House was shown to me. It involved providing a father figure to many children under one roof and teaching the love of God. I have told several people about it in detail since then and I found out about the ARK Program at the Dream Centre months later.

This all started with you, Bette. You are the inspiration that has touched so many and it is now spreading throughout the world. I hope this blesses you as much as you have blessed me. I love you.

PS: Please check out their website to see what God started through you — www.arkd.info.

Never too early, never too late to start

Imagine how I felt when I read this email! I was humbled and greatly blessed that God took my small offering of words and caring and used it in such a big way. The power of encouraging words to liberate grown-up kids makes me ask, "What would be the result if we started this practice when our children are little, giving them encouragement and help in reaching their own goals (instead of those we set for them)? What if we actively and intentionally encouraged them to recognize the gifts and talents they have?"

Your words are powerful!

Helping our kids identify their strengths and encouraging them to value their uniqueness is a strong foundation for their lives as adults. These would be the kind of kids who can dream and take action because they are standing strong on the foundation we have built for them.

Sadly, it seems there are so many kids (both young and grown) in today's culture who could use the extra encouragement in this area. The great news is that it is never too late to start this practice and reap the benefits in our lives!

What I learned was that it *starts* with me. The more I begin to recognize and take ownership of my uniqueness, strengths, and the value of my experiences, I can in turn reach out and offer this kind of encouragement to others. And so can you!

Vision and value

I can't remember ever answering the question, "What do you want to be when you grow up?" when I was young. In retrospect, perhaps it wasn't the culture in the 40s and 50s for parents to ask this question of their children, but if they did, I wasn't listening.

All I knew was that I wanted to grow up, get married, and have a baby. At age 16, that was just what I did. I didn't know anything about raising a child and I stumbled through being a parent and trying to support us with a few short-term, dead-end jobs. I was still a very strong-willed girl, trying to survive, with an added responsibility and no knowledge.

When I was 20, I married for the second time and ended up with a career raising five babies. During those years, I began to discover some of my own strengths. I found I had the talent to be an artist and an interior decorator. I took art classes and before long I became a leader in the art associations within my community.

I found I could be a good manager. With my husband gone for long periods of time, my strengths in time and resource management came out as I managed our busy household alone. I learned to problem solve, facilitate, referee (a very good skill to have with five children!), organize, and more!

It would seem with all the gifting that manifested in my life that I would have been a reasonably happy and fulfilled person. Not so, as you have read. Although I was recognizing some of my strengths in the midst of raising my family, I was still struggling to understand how to get my own needs met and take care of my kids. Underneath the outer shell lived a lonely person, desperate for love and meaning.

You can make choices out of security rather than out of fear and need.

Today, I understand that I can make choices based on knowing that the God who created me also designed me just as I am, including my strengths and passions ... just as He has you. This allows me to make choices from security rather than from fear and need. Realizing this has brought about a major shift in my life — it isn't about me anymore. It's about using my strengths, gifts, and experiences to serve God and others.

My experience of working through this personal process has shown me that everyone has a "lost" place inside and is looking for answers. You may be the answer for the person beside you. A hug or an affirming word or touch might make the life-changing difference for that person. Don't withhold what is within your power to give. Look for the good in others and be generous with your positive feedback and praise.

Seeing the real you

Early in my life, I didn't understand the concept of honoring. I have come to understand it more from the position of being dishonored! Being dishonored by being treated disrespectfully, with excessive criticism, only reinforced my negative belief in myself.

As I got older, I realized that those who had treated me like I was important to them had played a much bigger part in my life than I knew. When I felt honored (appreciated) or valued, I did better; I was challenged to stretch and believe I could be and do more.

When I felt no value or dishonored, I wanted to quit. I felt like I wasn't any good.

The "act" of honoring or dishonoring has incredible power. It can lift you to a new level where you can reach for more or it can leave you with emotional scars and baggage that weigh you down.

I really began to feel like a success when I was able to see myself through the eyes of others with whom I worked. I was a sales director in a major cosmetic company for several years. I did quite well, so well that I earned the cars given for meeting ambitious sales goals. However, the biggest reward was the transformation that happened when I saw my worth and value through the eyes of my associates.

Part of building success in this company was building a client base by asking people if I could give them facials to demonstrate the product. At first, all I could see out of my own eyes was my fear. *Why would anyone want to do a facial with me?* I wondered.

I found myself in a crisis of confidence. I had an internal belief I could be a leader in this company, so I joined with the goal to be a sales director and train women. The unique opportunities for women to grow and the chance to use my skills appealed to me.

Here is where my belief ran head on into my crisis of confidence!

Does your belief ever run into a crisis of confidence?

If I couldn't ask prospects if they wanted a facial, I wasn't much of a leader, was I? And how could I teach others to do what I couldn't do?

One day, all the area sales directors gathered around me and asked me what was keeping me from my goal. I told them, "No one would want to do a facial with me!"

They all laughed and said, "You don't realize who YOU are! Anyone would love to have a facial with you. You are fun, approachable, and are offering a treat! Women are waiting for you to ask. Go out and ask 20 people and see what happens. See them as really wanting to say 'yes' to you."

Well, I did! Guess what? They were right! The more I asked and people said "yes," the more I was built up inside. My confidence grew and I began to really know and believe that I could do it! Just six months later, I was a sales director. My gorgeous pale pink director's outfit showed the world I was a winner. I looked just like the other leaders and top people in the company.

When it came my turn to go to the home of the founder of the company and have my picture taken with her, I knew that I could do anything I decided to do. It was a major step ahead for me. I had stepped out of my insecurities, found a new confidence, and achieved an ambitious goal. This moment was a transformational experience in my life. A new vision for my future was open to me because others in my life had enabled me to see my own value with their encouraging words.

Sharing the wealth

It would seem like knowing the significant effect of our words, both positive and negative, would dramatically change the way we interact. I've found it does have an effect, but as human beings, we are weak and susceptible to feelings ... those of our own and especially those of others. Unless you've come to a place of strong confidence and discipline (I'm still working on getting there, too), it is easy to lapse into old practices or respond selfishly.

When I became clear about my goals and connected to something larger than myself, I was able to create a compelling mission statement that not only inspired me, it reminded me to share the wealth of grace and kindness through my words that had been extended to me. My actual mission statement is: "I am a people builder."

The way I live my mission statement is: "Developing Leaders with A Passion to Make a Difference in the World." One of my favorite things about this is that it lets me channel my passion and experience into others and applies to all of my relationships. This includes my family, my associates, my community, my friends, and even friends I haven't met yet!

My family has changed ... because I changed. As the kids have grown up, I've seen changes beyond my wildest dreams. My daughters, Kathie and Patsi, entrepreneurs in their own right, are some of my best friends and business advisors. My oldest and youngest sons, Mick and David, are successful business owners as well. Our relationship reflects the rich love and respect gained from the hard road we've traveled. My son, Kevin, is an exceptional father and entrepreneur. I respect his talent and the strength of his resolve as he creates the life of his dreams with his little family.

Most of my grandchildren and I now communicate fairly often. My newest role as great-grandmother has me more aware than ever of ways to be involved. I attribute the change in our relationships to being fully engaged in life and the lives of those around me, believing the best in them and communicating that message in any way I can.

Note: Another key element I'd be remiss if I didn't mention is my newfound ability to ask for forgiveness. During the initial period of my re-awakening, I came to understand how my own issues had affected my children. Not only did I need to forgive hurtful things said and done over the years, I needed to confess my own shortcomings and ask for forgiveness in return. This was an important and necessary step in living my outrageous life. Taking time to intentionally build, repair, and nurture relationships has become a new priority, and that includes choosing to offer and ask for forgiveness.

With these changes in my attitude toward others, my nutritional business flourished. I experienced business growth that continues to be a blessing and attests to the positive transformation of my life. My passion to make a difference in people's lives through better health attracted others of like mind who wanted to work with me or those on my team.

As a result, I found a way to multiply my passion by investing in and training leaders for the next generation. There's no magic formula for building a successful organization regardless of your business model. It simply takes vision, focus, and consistent commitment to activities that get results.

Live life with intention and purpose!

My world expanded beyond my own small circle when I decided to live life with intention and purpose. Yours can too. It probably won't look a lot like mine, but it only needs to look like a life that will inspire and engage you.

Without vision, we die. Use our Outrageous Life Design Tool in Chapter 9 to stretch your thinking and tap into the desires of your heart. I am blessed to have realized the error of my thinking at age 66, but it is never too early or late to start!

What about you?

Are there areas of your life you've given up on? What changes can you make to create a different outcome?

1. When you were young, what did you want to be when you grew up? What is the essence of that calling? (i.e. service, counsel, building, exploring, creating)

2. How can you incorporate more of this calling into daily practice?

3. What are the three things you'd like to change about yourself today? Can you reflect on those three things and find the good in them?

You were given a life so you could live it. I pray this book has challenged you, made you laugh, and touched your heart. Most of all I hope it reminds you of the amazing gift you are and inspires you to create an outrageous over the top life all your own.

"He gave those who mourn a crown of beauty for ashes, a joyous blessing instead of mourning, festive praise instead of despair. In their righteousness, they will be like great oaks that the LORD has planted for his own glory" (Isaiah 61:3).

Chapter Nine

Kathie's Outrageous Life Design Tool

I've known my mom a long time — my whole life! Watching and being a part of her transformation continues to be inspirational. Don't think it has always been easy. If it weren't for my own experience and transformation journey, it might have taken me longer to appreciate hers.

You've heard a little of my story through my mom's eyes. As I've co-written each chapter and helped her distill the essential elements to share with you, I've come to an even greater understanding of her impact on who I am today.

I felt stuck for most of my life ... have you?

I felt stuck for most of my life. Almost as if I was viewing my experiences from outside my body. I felt different, like I didn't fit, like I wasn't good enough, could never be good enough, and destined to fall short.

Any of those phrases sound familiar to you? You probably have these or similar nagging "gremlins" hanging around your memory banks, too.

Early on I was imprinted with the message that it was not a good thing to be me. I say "imprinted" because even now that I know it's not true, I can still have a visceral response when I say the words out loud.

Are your success habits actually hurting you?

My parents, wrapped up in their own issues, had no idea this was the message they were conveying. I couldn't even articulate this simple phrase until a few years ago, but its affect on my life was significant. It was like an invisible filter on the choices I made and created a reality that I was desperate to leave behind.

Needless to say, most of my energy in life has been spent learning and adapting just to survive and fit in. Every day, every job, every relationship ... this was my pattern: Learn what was expected, adapt to be that person or role, and work hard to meet the expectation. This served me well as I could always rise quickly to the top in my work environments, but those patterns came at a tremendous cost to me and my family.

Having been weaned on princess stories, I will admit in the recesses of my heart I carried a wish that a knight on a white horse would come into my life, see me as beautiful, perfect, and endearing, and make all the struggle go away.

As I matured, this wish easily evolved into looking for a secret formula, silver bullet, or someone with a magic wand to wave all my worries away. Eventually, like Dorothy in *The Wizard of Oz*, I realized I had my own version of the ruby slippers — the ability to create the outrageous life of my dreams.

I had the power all along!

While you do hold the keys to your own transformation, the truth is that it's NOT an overnight makeover. I've heard it said that personal transformation is like peeling an onion. The outer layers come off the easiest. They are big and ugly and bring tears and sniffles. But it doesn't stop there. The closer to the heart, the layers are more transparent, are harder to peel, and bring real tears in abundance.

Here's a tool that helped me on my journey. It was a key element in tapping the power of the vision of my future ideal life and closing the gap between the negative actions and thoughts that were keeping me attaining that place of contentment and fulfillment. I trust in sharing my journey you'll be encouraged to take the first steps to creating your own outrageous life.

The outrageous life design tool

First step:

Understand this is YOUR life

We are whole people who have whole lives. We are not just mothers, daughters, wives, sisters, employees, business owners, or whatever title we feel most represents us. We have one life. This is IT. You were born wired to be YOU; with desires in your heart to fulfill your purpose and motivation to keep you going when you hit bumps in the road.

I may not be telling you anything you don't already know, but I want to give you permission today to fully engage with designing the life that your heart desires.

You may already be arguing with me, "But what about my kids, my spouse, or my workplace? They are disrespectful, make poor choices, and are irresponsible. I am already trying hard to be a good mom, wife, and worker. The changes that need to happen are bigger than me!"

I understand how you feel. I've felt the same way. What I've learned is that I can only change ME. When I changed, my environments began to change. My children changed. My spouse changed. I don't want to make it sound all magical, but when I changed, it started the process.

We are most frustrated by our unmet expectations — our own and those that others put upon us. When we reach a point of awareness, we are at the point of choice. We can choose to work around, adapt, or suppress our own desires ... or we can take the time to define and design outcomes that will be over the top or outrageous for our life experience.

Your choice!

My story: Before I had children, I promised myself I would never do to them what my parents did to me. Sound familiar? Specifically, I never wanted to let discipline degrade to a screaming match or have a divided approach to parenting with my husband. This all sounds good.

> Awareness is the first step toward change.

For those of you who are parents, you probably started the journey with similar ideals and aspirations. My boys were about 8 and 12 when I was made aware I'd never imagined fully what I wanted my interactions with my children to look like ... only what I didn't want them to look like. The end result was that I was a screaming maniac on occasion, with the voice in my head saying, "You are just like your mother!" And the kids played one parent against the other.

I became aware of this by a question that was asked of me. I was shown a tool and asked to be brutally honest, rating my satisfaction with my environment at home and my relationships on a scale of 1-10. When I took a good look, I had to admit some pretty low numbers.

The question that followed my honesty introspection was enlightening: "What characteristics or outcomes would make this area a 10?"

Like I've shared, I was so busy thinking about what I did NOT want that I had never really articulated or clarified my heart's desire.

What about you?

What follows is a tool that will be a guide to you as you check in with your current situation. Be honest with yourself. Don't rate your own fulfillment factors based on someone else's standards. If you've never created your own benchmarks, now is a great time to think about it!

This tool will help you:

1. Assess your current fulfillment factor

2. Envision what an outrageous life might look like for you

3. Plan steps to close the gaps between your current state and your ideal

Where do you start?

Copy wheel (on the following page) onto a blank piece of paper, write directly in the book, or write on the wheel provided in the back of this book.

Now, take a few minutes and think about each segment of life identified here. Rate each area on a scale of 1-10 (1 is low, 10 is high).

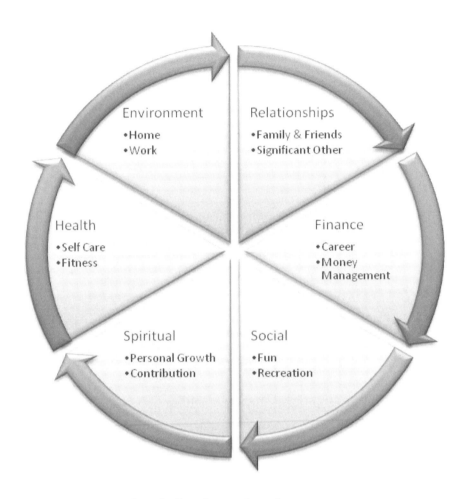

Put a point on a "spoke" or line of each segment as you rate your current satisfaction in each area. A zero would put the point right at the center of the wheel, while a 10 would put it at the edge.

This is not the time to assign guilt about what you think you should be doing or having, but rather, this is a time to focus on reality.

Be honest about where you are right now, knowing that you can start moving closer to where you want to be.

My Story: My first attempt at this tool illustrated a very bumpy wheel. My life was totally out of balance according to most standards. I was more satisfied in work than in any other area of my life.

This wasn't surprising since, I spent most of my time and energy thinking about that area of my life. As I mentioned above, this life design assessment clearly showed my focus and gave me opportunity to choose to adjust my time and clarify my expectations.

Using this tool in the early 90s, I rated both my environment and my family relationship satisfaction in the 3-4 range, lower than I wanted. My next step was to define the characteristics that would make it ideal or over the top.

Here are a few of my answers. (Note: I wrote my answers to combine my core beliefs and the ideal as if it were the current state.)

1. Relationships: I believe my children are individuals gifted with their own combination of strengths and talents. It is my responsibility to create an environment conducive to their growth.

    a. My home is a place of tranquility, safety, and mutual respect.

    b. My children feel valued through their surroundings, my time, and communication.

    c. I respect my children. I honor their contribution to our home, to their school, to their friends, and to the community.

2. I believe this looks like:

    a. My house is in order. Each person is responsible for maintaining his or her own area.

b. When any family member leaves or returns, the communication is focused on transitioning well, communicating love and appreciation.

c. I am interested in what they are interested in: their friends, hobbies, homework, sports, books, games, etc. I make time to get updates and encourage those interests.

d. I seek to find the positive in every situation. I invest time to learn character qualities and their misuse so I can acknowledge the strength instead of focusing on the negative expression.

e. I strive not to impose my expectations of success on my family but rather to have open communication where I can learn more about them as individuals, their hopes, and dreams.

I began defining my outrageous life on purpose over 15 years ago. The immediate effect was apparent in my home and in my communication with my children. When they would experience frustration at school or not complete their homework, rather than making demands about changing the behavior, I began to ask questions, acknowledging their approach (whether positive or negative), and affirming the positive characteristic I saw in them.

> When I changed, everything around me changed ... and I could have made that change many years earlier!

Our home quickly became more tranquil. The only thing that had changed was *me* and the *choices I made* after defining what I wanted in an ideal environment (to download "Discerning Positive Character Traits in Negative Behavior," visit our website www.IWantWhatShesGotSecrets.com).

An outrageous life is truly yours to define. It can start here.

ttnogool

Before you think that I had a head start, I want you to see my own wheel. Below is what my wheel looked like:

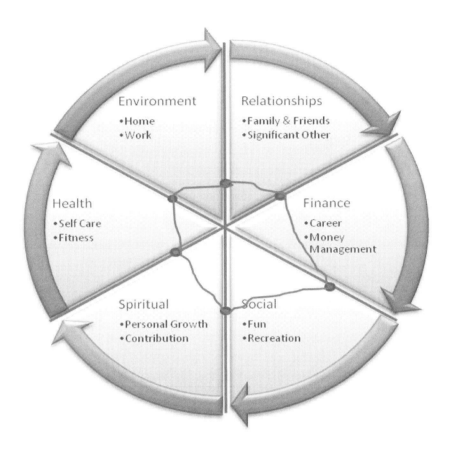

I'm quick to admit that my wheel would never have gone very fast, but I chose to change, and it's paid great dividends!

As it is with any journey, you need to find your starting place first. The next step is the task of picturing where you want to go.

Let's take Step 2:

Envision your own outrageous life.

I first experimented with this tool in my 30s. My kids were young, I worked full time, and I was stressed. When the speaker told me I could have the life of my dreams, I laughed! I thought I'd already made the choices that set my path for the rest of my life. Years later, I've used this tool myself as well as with countless clients. It's always the same. Starting with unbelief, a person gradually moves to empowerment as the evidence of the power of vision and small steps is made real.

Unbelief becomes empowerment as vision and small action steps take place.

On another blank sheet of paper, or on the extra wheels in the back of the book, copy the wheel with the areas of your life again. Think about the characteristics of a life that would be outrageous to you.

A quick exercise is to take each segment of the wheel and write some key words and phrases. If you'd like to deepen the learning, plan some time to be in a quiet place and ask yourself the following questions.

1. When I envision the ideal state in this area (Family, Career, Finance, Health, Spirituality, Environment, Social)

   a. What does it look like? (i.e. When I come into my home it looks like … I see …)

   b. What does it sound like? (i.e. When I come into my home it sounds like … I hear … I say …)

   c. What does it feel like? (i.e. To me it feels … It feels like this to others …)

Here is a quick overview of some of the key words and phrases in my first wheel:

- Family — a home without screaming, where my children felt valued and empowered.

- Environment — a house where there was order instead of chaos, made beds and clean kitchen.

- Work/Career — working hours that allowed me personal and family time.

More recent key words and phrases in recent exercises are:

- Family/friends — harmonious relationships, regular visits to see extended family and friends, quality face time with each child and my husband on a regular basis.

- Environment — a home where guests feel welcomed and valued, filled with joy and laughter, travel to exotic locations for work and leisure, warm weather.

- Work/Career — Teaching, Speaking, Coaching; see my work as contribution, working in my strengths.

What about you? You may feel like your dreams could never become reality. This is your time — let your imagination go! The sky's the limit! How would your life be different?

Wrap up with Step 3:

Close the gap

Now that your juices are flowing and ideas are popping, take the time to focus and identify what might get in your way.

I selected my home and my family to start the transformation because they needed the most attention. Through this process, I could see that small shifts in behavior, attitude, and communication could make significant change.

What about you? Is there an area or two on your life design tool that stood out to you as needing immediate attention? Take your blank sheet of paper where you rated your current life against your ideal. Add to your notes.

1. Identify 1-3 things you could do right now that would move you closer to your outrageous life.

2. Set a goal with a date to implement the action items you identified.

3. Write down what might get in your way.

   a. Don't know enough about …

   b. Need to contact someone …

   c. Person in my life …

4. Make a plan to resolve obstacles.

   a. If you don't know enough about something, reach out and ask someone who does.

   b. If you need to make some connections, do the research to find out who to talk to or how to take your next step.

   c. If you are dealing with a difficult person, ask for help. Seek counsel. Ask others how they've dealt with this issue.

You have the power to make choices that will move you to your ideal life. It can be a challenge to overcome some of the past influences that have made you settle for less in your life, but it's never too late to start! The journey starts with taking one step at a time as you bring balance to areas of your life that are out of alignment.

Each of us has a responsibility to continue to refine and develop our strengths so we can bring our unique brilliance to our relationships, and the world.

Time is all we have. Our relationships are critical.

To fully experience an outrageous life we need to stay on top of those things that serve to move us forward and avoid those that create "drag" and hold us back from who we are innately wired to be.

Time ... is all you have.

I trust you will use the tools I've adapted through experience and my work in executive coaching to begin a new phase of transformation for yourself.

An over-the-top outrageous life is not just for others, it can be yours too.

End of the day—my outrageous life asssessment

7 Questions Every Woman Must Ask and Answer

1. **Purpose** — Why am I here? How do I live my life with purpose?

   a. What should I be doing more of? Less of?

   b. What is the current focus of my life? What do I want it to be?

   c. What legacy do I want to leave?

2. **Gift Mix** — What talents or value can I bring to the party besides my famous jello salad?

107

a. What are my strengths and talents? How do I use them in my life? (Suggested Resource: StrengthsFinders 2.0, Tom Rath)

b. Who can I ask for honest feedback?

c. How do I use my gifts and talents to serve others? If I can't readily think of any examples, what are some ways I could add this to my life?

3. **Relationships** — How can I make the time I spend with friends and family count?

a. Do I have a trusted group of friends? If not, how will I add these people in my life?

b. What activities do I need to eliminate that drain me and make it difficult to connect with others?

c. Are there people in my life who don't support or encourage me? How can I make positive changes in these relationships?

4. **Contribution** — Beyond warming the couch cushions, watching the grand-kids and playing bridge — what difference can I make?

a. Do I give back to worthy causes? Which ones?

b. What causes interest me? Children, orphans, homeless, troops, Habitat for Humanity, disaster areas, etc.

c. What is a first step I could take to get involved in my community?

5. **Self-Care** — Does my health affect my outlook and energy? Do I take the time to do what I need to do for me?

    a. How can I make positive changes to my diet and plan for meals that sustain me?

    b. What are the activities that feed my soul? Art, music, recreation? How can I plan time for these?

    c. How can I take better care of my body?

6. **Vision** — Beyond what I can see with my bifocals — what's in store for the rest of my life?

    a. Do I have a long term plan? Have I checked it recently?

    You can have the outrageous life that you want!

    b. At the end of my life (which isn't now) what do I want those around me to say about me?

    c. Is there something that stirs my heart but I've decided I am too old to accomplish? Who's telling me I can't? Why?

7. **Spirituality** — Knowing that soul care is an important part of living the outrageous life, how do I feed my spirit?

    a. Do I engage in a search for spiritual nourishment in my life? Where do I go when I need to connect with something bigger than myself?

    b. Do I have a practice that feeds and energizes my spiritual side?

      c. Do I really understand the significance of my own life and feel a higher purpose? How does that demonstrate itself in my life?

The words of the insightful song, "Legacy," follow. Take just a moment to read and ponder:

LEGACY
by Nichole Nordeman

Don't mind if you've got something nice to say about me
And I enjoy an accolade like the rest
And you could take my picture and hang it in a gallery
Of all the Who's Who's and So-and-So's
That used to be the best at such and such
It wouldn't matter much

I won't lie, it feels alright to see your name in lights
We all need an "Atta boy" or "Atta girl"
But in the end I'd like to hang my hat on more besides
The temporary trappings of this world

I want to leave a legacy
How will they remember me?
Did I choose to love?
Did I point to You enough?
To make a mark on things
I want to leave an offering
A child of mercy and grace
Who blessed Your name unapologetically
And leave that kind of legacy

Don't have to look too far or too long awhile
To make a lengthy list of all that I enjoy
It's an accumulating trinket and a treasure pile
Where moth and rust, thieves and such will soon enough destroy

Not well-traveled, not well-read
Not well-to-do, or well-bred
Just want to hear instead
Well done, good and faithful one

I don't mind if you've got something nice to say about me

Lyrics by Nicole Nordeman Copyright © 2002 Ariose Music (ASCAP) (adm. at EMICMGPublishing.com) All rights reserved. Used by permission.

Epilogue

a note from Bette

As I wrote this book, I had you in mind. I suggest you take this time to slow down to enjoy, learn, and process. I am honored that you chose to spend some time with me.

Unlike many my age, the pace of my life is a little faster these days. At 73, I've found my sweet spot and try to stay right in its center. This makes some a little uncomfortable. I hear comments that range from, "Bette, don't you think you should slow down? Don't you need more balance in your life? Don't you think you are going to wear yourself out?" I have to chuckle to myself. In the past I might have said the same things to someone like me ... what I know now is that each of us has our own set point for pace and capacity. Stretching and living full out is what makes this journey an adventure!

I've been raising eyebrows most of my life. As a child, I remember going to the movies with my mother. At the close of the show (as they did in those days) the announcer promoted a talent show in the coming weeks. When he asked for participants, I was half way down the aisle before my mother caught the back of my jumper and asked, "What do you think you are doing?" I told her I was going to perform. She asked what I planned to do. I said "I will figure it out when I get there." This was an early indicator of things to come.

Like many of you I started out with a strong belief in myself. Most of us do. After years of adapting to the world around me and many blows gained in the school of hard knocks I settled into mediocrity and battered self-esteem. This short book is a compilation of lessons and observations learned the hard way. I've added some food for thought to stretch you and encourage you to live your own life … outrageously!

— Bette James Laughrun

a note from Kathie

Co-authoring this book with my mom has been an outrageous adventure in and of itself. When I've shared about this project in my community the usual response is one of awe. Many respond with "I could NEVER write a book with my mother. We'd end up killing each other in the process!" Writing this has never been like that for me. You see, I lived through most of the experiences my mom is drawing on from her learning which gives me a unique perspective. My experience as a leadership and executive coach was essential to capture the nuggets we share.

Honestly, most of my life the relationship with my mom was strained to non-existent. Her low self-esteem expressed toward me took its toll in my formative years. It took my own journeys of self-discovery and personal breakthrough to be able to see who I truly was and in turn to see the truth about her struggle. My personal breakthroughs began in my mid-30s, hers in her mid-60s. This goes to show you it is never too late to become what you were created for!

I believe this book will be a catalyst for many. It is so easy to lose hope in our current environment. The negative messages, continual comparison to others who we perceive as being more successful and powerful than we, all compound an already wounded self esteem. It's time for a fresh voice! It's time for women who've transformed their lives from mediocre to outrageous to speak out! My mom is one of those women! She is a woman of courage, vision, and tenacity. I trust you will be inspired to find your own breakthrough and choose to live your own outrageous life … everyday!

— Kathie (Laughrun) Nelson

Outrageous Life Resources

Chapter 1: Life Is a Choice
- Klemmer and Associates (Klemmer.com) (I challenge you to experience one of these transformational leadership and personal development seminars.)
- *When Good Intentions Run Smack into Reality*, Brian Klemmer
- *The Compassionate Samurai*, Brian Klemmer (Brian's books are great how-to's and a must have for any library.)

Chapter 2: Outrageous Living Is Supernatural
- *Beyond Ourselves*, by Catherine Marshall (My parents sent me this wonderful book that helped me make the transition to calling out to God for help a reality.)
- *Mere Christianity*, C.S. Lewis
- *The Heart of the Five Love Languages*, Gary Chapman. (This is an excellent resource to understand the language of appreciation and love.)
- www.needhim.org and 888-NEED-HIM (6333-446) (Check out this great resource that answers common, faith questions.)
- *A White Stone*, Jim Corbett (A dynamic, suspenseful, powerful novel about how God changed an inner-city man's life.)

Chapter 3: The Cost of Love
- Discerning Positive Character Qualities in Negative Behavior Traits (You can download this directly from our site www.IWantWhatShesGotSecrets.com)

Chapter 4: Leadership: Watering the Seeds of Greatness
- Dr. Myles Munroe (Discover your purpose in life and overcome obstacles to your vision. Dr. Munroe has amazing insight into your gifts and your destiny. These are my favorites:
    - *In Charge*
    - *The Spirit of Leadership*
    - *The Power of Vision*

Chapter 5: The Power of Contribution
- *Jerusalem*, Collins and Lapierre (An epic drama of 1948. An account of that period encompassing the full spectrum of its participants, their experiences, emotions, and acts of bravery.)
- *From Time Immemorial*, Peters (The origins of the Arab-Jewish conflict over Palestine.)
- *Celebrating Jesus in the Biblical Feasts: Discovering Their Significance to You as a Christian* by Richard Booker
- International Christian Embassy Jerusalem, www.icej.org (Info on how, why and where you can celebrate the Biblical Feasts.)

Chapter 6: Surviving Contradiction
- *7 Habits of Highly Effective People*, Stephen Covey (This book was a life changer for me when I thought having a job was the only way to earn a living. I found my life purpose and mission statement as a result of this fine book.)
- *Awakening the Entrepreneur Within*, Michael Gerber
- *E-Myth Revisited*, Michael Gerber (Gerber's books are a must for every entrepreneur or self employed person.)

Chapter 7: Living a Healthy, Outrageous Life
- Isagenix, www.thepeoplebuilders.isagenix.com (My personal business address.)
- Online video: "Are you toxic" at above address. Go to IsaVideos at the top of page.

Chapter 8: A New Beginning
- *The Go Giver*, Bob Burg and John David Mann
- *Go-Givers Sell More*, Bob Burg and John David Mann (These two books embody the philosophy of sales that I teach.)
- www.ThePeopleBuilders.com my blog and book site.

Chapter 9: Kathie's Outrageous Life Design Tool
- StrengthsFinder 2.0, Tom Rath
- StrengthsExplorer For Ages 10 to 14: From Gallup, the Creators of StrengthsFinder
- Discerning Positive Character Qualities in Negative Behavior Traits (You can download directly from our site www.IWantWhatShesGotSecrets.com)
- *The Purpose Driven Life*, Rick Warren

NOTES

NOTES

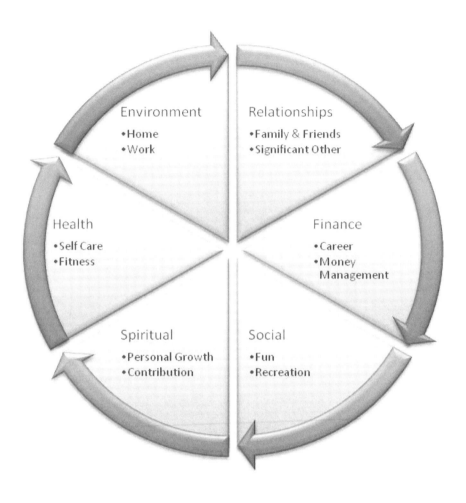

122

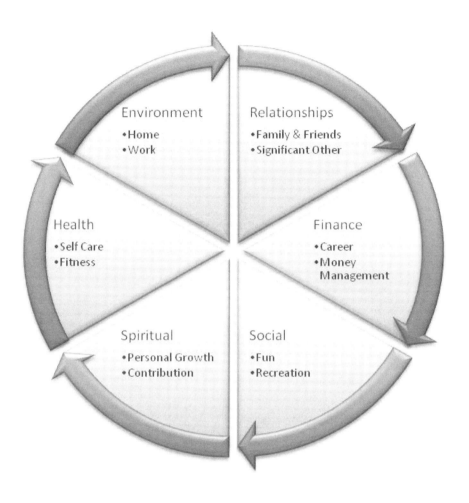

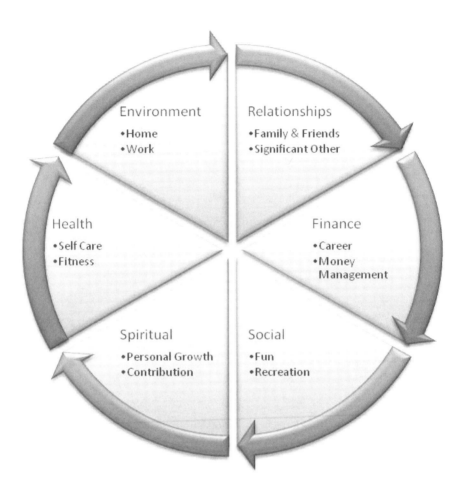

124

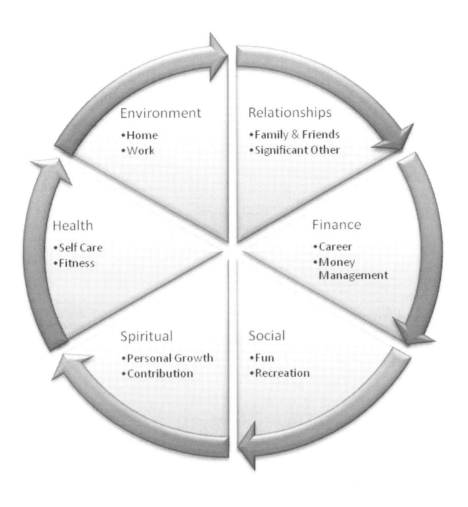

To order your copy of

I WANT WHAT SHE'S GOT!
— THE SECRETS OF CREATING AN OUTRAGEOUS LIFE

VISIT WWW.IWANTWHATSHESGOTSECRETS.COM

OR CALL 1-800-728-1779